ACADEMIC WORD POWER 2

ACADEMIC WORD POWER 2

Celia Thompson
Series Editor: Donna Obenda
University of North Texas

HEINLE
CENGAGE Learning™

Australia • Brazil • Japan • Korea • Mexico • Singapore • Spain • United Kingdom • United States

Academic Word Power 2
Celia Thompson
Series Editor: Donna Obenda

Editor in Chief: Patricia A. Coryell

Director of ESL Publishing: Susan Maguire

Senior Development Editor:
    Kathleen Sands-Boehmer

Editorial Assistant: Evangeline Bermas

Cover Design manager: Diana Coe

Marketing Manager: Annamarie Rice

ISBN-13: 978-0-618-39769-3

ISBN-10: 0-618-39769-8

Heinle
20 Channel Center Street
Boston, MA 02210
USA

Cengage Learning is a leading provider of customized learning solutions with office locations around the globe, including Singapore, the United Kingdom, Australia, Mexico, Brazil, and Japan. Locate your local office at **www.cengage.com/global**

Cengage Learning products are represented in Canada by Nelson Education, Ltd.

Visit Heinle online at **elt.heinle.com**

Visit our corporate website at **www.cengage.com**

Printed in the United States of America
10 11 12 13 14   21 20 19 18 17

CONTENTS

UNIT 3

WORDS

alternative	emerge	license	reject
constant	external	medical	style
contribution	fundamental	modify	sum
corresponding	image	option	sustainable
dominant	investigation	project	transition

UNIT 4

WORDS

apparent	domestic	integration	proportion
aware	ethnic	logic	resolution
clause	evolution	network	sufficient
considerable	grant	objective	symbolic
decline	instance	overall	version

UNIT 5

WORDS

adjustment	convention	hypothesis	notion
author	display	intelligence	orientation
brief	equivalent	lecture	pursue
civil	fee	liberal	statistic
commitment	flexibility	minimum	stability

UNIT 6

WORDS

adequate	draft	justification	revenue
attach	expert	monitor	status
capacity	furthermore	perspective	substitution
consultation	ignored	precise	trend
dimension	instruction	prime	welfare

UNIT 7

WORDS

access	criteria	parallel	shift
accurate	discretion	principal	subsequent
concentration	implementation	promote	summary
consent	imposed	retain	undertake
coordination	marginal	scheme	volume

INTRODUCTION

WELCOME TO *ACADEMIC WORD POWER*!

ACADEMIC WORD POWER is a four-volume vocabulary series for students of English at the high school or college level who are planning to pursue further academic studies. The goal of the series is to help students learn the vocabulary they need for success in academic reading and writing.

ACADEMIC WORD POWER 1 is designed for intermediate students.

ACADEMIC WORD POWER 2, 3, and *4* are designed for high-intermediate, advanced, and high-advanced levels, respectively.

The target vocabulary in all four volumes was selected from the Academic Word List (AWL) developed by Averil Coxhead in 1998. The AWL, which contains 570 words, was compiled from a corpus of 3.5 million words found in academic texts. When students add the words from this list to a basic vocabulary of 2000 words, they will be able to comprehend approximately 90 percent of the vocabulary in academic texts. When proper nouns and technical vocabulary are added to this, students approach the 95 percent comprehension level that research has shown is needed for successful academic reading.

TO THE TEACHER . . .

Series Approach

Reflecting the latest research in vocabulary acquisition and pedagogy, the exercises and activities in this text are based on an interactive approach to vocabulary instruction. Consequently, the reading, writing and speaking exercises give the student multiple exposures to the target words in meaningful contexts and provide rich information about each word. The exercises also establish ties between the target words and the student's prior knowledge and experience.

About the Books

Each volume has seven units that target 20 AWL words per unit. Thus, 140 AWL words are studied in each book, and 560 of the 570 words on the AWL are covered in the four volumes. The AWL words were sequenced and grouped into the four volumes by taking into consideration the frequency of the words, their level of difficulty and the thematic relationships between the words. A great variety of vocabulary development practice activities as well as strategies for learning and remembering academic vocabulary are incorporated in each book.

Text Organization

The seven units in each book are divided into four lessons that focus on five AWL words. Every lesson includes the following components:

- **Word Families**: This section introduces the five target words by providing a head word, which is the most frequently used in academic texts, as well as other word forms of the target word. A chart is provided for students to place the different word forms under the correct part of speech. This focus on word families helps students decipher new words and build spelling proficiency.

- **Reading**: A one-paragraph reading introduces students to the five target words in an academic context.

- **Comprehension Check**: Two exercises check students' superficial comprehension of the target words. For the first exercise, students match definitions by using the context provided in the reading in the previous section. The second exercise includes exercises such as true/false statements, yes/no questions, odd man out, fill in the blank, or matching sentence halves.

- **Word Study**: This section provides rich instruction through exercises that offer an expansion of the target words. This is accomplished through a wide variety of exercises, such as collocations, multiple meanings, grammar application, word form practice, analogies, pronunciation tips, and idiomatic usage. Both the written exercises in this section and the previous section are designed to be completed quickly by students and graded easily by teachers because research shows that the type of written exercise is not significant in terms of retention. Rather, it is the number of retrievals that is significant. Thus, it is better to have a larger quantity of exercises that can be done quickly as opposed to a smaller number of exercises that are time-consuming to complete (such as writing original sentences with the target words).

- **Using Words in Communication:** Communicative activities in this section give students practice in using the target words fluently. The students use the target words orally in different settings, such as sentence completion, discussion, role-play, interviewing, summarizing, paraphrasing, storytelling, listing ideas related to the target word, or associating the target word with other words from the unit. These activities aid in retention of the target words as they develop a link between the target words and students' past experience and knowledge.

Other features of the series include:

- **Unit Reviews:** Each unit ends with an exercise that reviews all 20 words from the unit through an easy-to-do, fun activity, such as a crossword puzzle, find-a-word, word scramble, sentence scramble, associations, and definition match-up.

- **Website:** All four volumes have a companion website with an instructor and student site. This site can be accessed at elt.thomson.com/wordpower. The instructor site includes unit assessments and the answer key for the book. The student site includes longer readings with the target AWL words, vocabulary flashcards, and review quizzes for each lesson.

- **Easy to supplement with writing activities:** If a teacher wants to do more extensive writing practice with the target words, the books can be easily supplemented with writing activities such as writing original sentences, paragraphs and essays with the AWL words.

TO THE STUDENT . . .

Did you know the following facts?

- The average native English-speaking university student has a vocabulary of around 21,000 words.

- The average adult ESL student learns about 2,500 English words per year.

Before you get depressed and discouraged, consider the following fact: English (like any other language) uses a relatively small number of words over and over again. Words that are used over and over again are called "high frequency" words. The words you will be studying in this book come from a high frequency list called the *Academic Word List* (AWL). The AWL contains 570 words that frequently occur in academic texts, such as university textbooks, course workbooks, and academic journal articles.

Why is it a good use of your time and energy to learn the words on the AWL?

If you add the 570 words on the AWL list to a basic vocabulary of 2000 English words (which most intermediate readers already have), you'll be able to understand 90% of the words in an average academic text. This book will help you learn many of the words on the AWL through numerous written exercises that introduce you to the meanings of the words and provide important information about the words, such as word forms, idiomatic uses, and pronunciation tips. This book also has many speaking activities that will give you practice using the new words fluently.

Besides completing all the exercises in the book, it is recommended that you use vocabulary cards to help you remember the new words. On the next page are some tips (advice) on how to make vocabulary cards.

HOW TO MAKE YOUR OWN VOCABULARY CARDS

1. Use small cards (no bigger than 3 by 5 inch) so that they can be easily carried.

2. Put the new word on one side and the definition (meaning) on the other side.

3. In addition to the definition, you can include the following information on the back side of the card:

    *   a translation of the new word in your language;
    *   pictures or diagrams related to the new word;
    *   phonetic pronunciation;
    *   a sample sentence using the new word.

4. Practice with the cards by looking at the new word and trying to recall the meaning first, and then (later) by looking at the meaning and trying to recall the new word.

5. Say the words aloud or to yourself when you are studying the cards.

6. Study the cards frequently. When you learn a new word, try to study it later that day, the next day, the next week, and then a few weeks later.

7. Study the words with a partner occasionally. When reviewing with a partner, try to use the word in a new sentence.

8. Change the order of the cards frequently. Don't order the cards alphabetically or put the cards in groups of similar words. Words which look the same or have similar meanings are easy to confuse.

GUIDE TO PRONUNCIATION

Vowels

Symbol	Key Word	Pronunciation
/ɑ/	hot	/hɑt/
/æ/	cat	/kæt/
/aɪ/	tie	/taɪ/
/aʊ/	cow	/kaʊ/
/ɛ/	bed	/bɛd/
/eɪ/	same	/seɪm/
/i/	he	/hɪ/
/ɪ/	it	/ɪt/
/oʊ/	go	/goʊ/
/ʊ/	book	/bʊk/
/ɔ/	dog	/dɔg/
/ɔɪ/	boy	/bɔɪ/
/ʌ/	cup	/kʌp/
/ɜr/	bird	/bɜrd/
/ə/	about	/əˈbaʊt/
	softer	/ˈsɔftər/

Consonants

Symbol	Key Word	Pronunciation
/b/	be	/bi/
/d/	did	/dɪd/
/dʒ/	jump	/dʒʌmp/
/f/	fat	/fæt/
/g/	go	/goʊ/
/h/	hit	/hɪt/
/k/	cat	/kæt/
/l/	life	/laɪf/
/m/	me	/mi/
/n/	no	/noʊ/
/ŋ/	sing	/sɪŋ/
/p/	pen	/pɛn/
/r/	red	/rɛd/
/s/	see	/si/
/t/	tea	/ti/
/tʃ/	cheap	/tʃip/
/v/	vote	/voʊt/
/w/	we	/wi/
/z/	zoo	/zu/
/ð/	they	/ðeɪ/
/θ/	thin	/θɪn/

GUIDE TO SYLLABLE STRESS

/ˈ/   open   /ˈoʊpən/
used before a syllable to show primary stress

/ˌ/   doorway   /ˈdɔrˌweɪ/
used before a syllable to show secondary stress

ACKNOWLEDGEMENTS

Many thanks to Averil Coxhead for giving us permission to use the *Academic Word List* (AWL) in the development of this series. It is hard to imagine the hours of planning and labor that went into compiling this list from such an extensive corpus (3.5 million running words from over 400 academic texts). For more information about the AWL see the article *A New Academic Word List* by Averil Coxhead in the Summer 2000 TESOL Quarterly.

Also, thanks to Barbara Hefka, an instructor at the University of North Texas Intensive English Language Institute (IELI) for sequencing and grouping the 570 words on the AWL for the four volumes in this series. When sequencing these words, Barbara had to take in consideration the frequency of the words, their level of difficulty, and thematic relationships between the words. It was a herculean task that only someone with Barbara's breadth of ESL experience and teaching intuition could have handled so well.

Huge thanks go to Judith Kulp, a publishing coordinator at UNT, for her invaluable, professional input on this project. Thanks also go to M. J. Weaver for her production skills, and to Yun Ju Kim, a communication design student at UNT, who created the graphics for the series.

Finally, thanks to Eva Bowman, Director of the IELI, and Dr. Rebecca Smith-Murdock, Director of International Programs, for their support in the development of the series. They had faith in my vision for the series and in the writing and creative abilities of the four authors: Lisa Hollinger, Celia Thompson, Pat Bull, and Barbara Jones.

- Donna Obenda

Many thanks go to Donna Obenda, without whose vision, guidance, and persistence these books would never have been written.

Thanks also go to my husband Tesfaye and daughter Zelalem, who keep me centered and focused.

- Celia Thompson

UNIT 1

WORDS

alter	energy	job	professional
annual	ensure	label	series
challenge	goal	mental	source
demonstrate	imply	outcome	stress
despite	illustrate	predict	target

READINGS

Professional Stress
The Challenge of Advertising
A Seamstress
Men's Favorite Magazine

STRATEGIES AND SKILLS

Word Forms
- Word family charts
- Word form selection

Comprehension Check
- Matching definitions
- Identifying synonyms
- Understanding and using words in context

Word Expansion
- Multiple meanings
- Collocations
- Suffixes

Interactive Speaking Practice
- Listing
- Sentence Completion
- Role play

ACADEMIC WORD POWER

LESSON 1

A. WORD FAMILIES

Study the five word families below. Then fill in the word form chart. The underlined word forms at the top of the list are the most commonly used forms in academic texts.

source	stress (2X)*	energy	label (2X)*	professional (2X)*
/sɔrs/	/strɛs/	/ˈɛnərdʒi/	/ˈleɪbəl/	/prəˈfɛʃənəl/
	stressful	energetic		profession
	stressed	energetically		professionally
	unstressed			professionalism

* used 2 times in the word form chart

Exercise - Word Form Chart

NOUN	VERB	ADJECTIVE	ADVERB
1. source			
1. stress	1.	1. 2. 3.	
1. energy		1.	1.
1. label	1.		
1. 2. 3.		1. professional	1.

B. READING

Professional Stress

A major <u>source</u> of <u>stress</u> for professionals in today's world is working against deadlines. It is expected that each person in an organization behaves <u>professionally</u>, which necessitates turning in assignments on time. Often managers push an employee to meet unrealistic deadlines; for instance, a boss might demand a week's worth of work in two days' time. If a worker fails to meet the deadline, he or she might be given the <u>label</u> of "slacker," or someone who doesn't put enough <u>energy</u> into his work. As a result, being a <u>professional</u> in today's world can be extremely stressful.

C. COMPREHENSION CHECK
Exercise 1
Refer to the reading above and use the context to guess the meanings of the words below. Then match the words to their definitions. Do NOT use a dictionary.

____ 1. source   A. capacity for much activity
____ 2. stress   B. beginning; cause
____ 3. energy   C. a short word or phrase describing a person, group, or thing
____ 4. label   D. a person who is expert at his or her work
____ 5. professional   E. mental or physical strain or difficulty caused by pressure

Exercise 2
Which word does not belong?

1.	source	origin	conclusion	supplier
2.	stress	relaxation	intensity	anxiety
3.	energy	power	vigor	calm
4.	label	name	picture	title
5.	professional	amateur	specialist	authority

D. WORD STUDY
Exercise 1
Most words have more than one meaning. Consider the various meanings of the word **stress**.

1.	stress (v) - to emphasize; to pronounce with prominent loudness; accent
2.	stress (n) - importance or significance attached to a thing; emphasis
3.	stress (n) - a specific response by the body to a stimulus, such as fear or pain; physical, mental, or emotional strain or tension
4.	stress (n) - the physical pressure, pull, or force exerted on one thing by another

Read the sentences below and decide if the meaning is 1, 2, 3, or 4.

____ 1. I have been under a lot of <u>stress</u> at work, because I'm working on a big, important project.
____ 2. I cannot <u>stress</u> the importance of this project enough.
____ 3. When you put <u>stress</u> on the wrong syllable, you can completely mispronounce a word and confuse your listener.
____ 4. The architects said the crack in the bridge was the result of <u>stress</u> from too much traffic.
____ 5 When I was a child, my mother always <u>stressed</u> the importance of getting a good education.
____ 6. His doctor told him to take a vacation because he had too much <u>stress</u> in his life.

Exercise 2

Choose the correct word form for each blank.

1. I hate my job. I never have any free time, so it's very _____.
   a. stress   b. stressful   c. stressed

2. Last Saturday night was fun. I danced so _____ I thought I might fly away.
   a. energetically   b. energy   c. energetic

3. It is difficult for a student to make a good impression after his teachers _____ him a troublemaker.
   a. labeling   b. label   c. labeled

4. Athletes who compete in the Olympics are not supposed to be _____ athletes.
   a. professionally   b. professional   c. professionalism

E. USING WORDS IN COMMUNICATION
Exercise 1

1. List 3 <u>sources</u> of information you might use in a research project.
2. List 3 things that make you feel <u>stressed</u>.
3. List 3 <u>sources</u> of <u>energy</u> besides oil and gas.
4. List 3 <u>labels</u> which are given to students.
5. List 3 <u>professional</u> sports teams.

Exercise 2

1. Describe a person you know who is very <u>energetic</u>.
2. How would you <u>label</u> yourself?
3. Describe a <u>stressful</u> day in your life.
4. Who in your life is a <u>source</u> of inspiration for you?
5. Describe <u>professional</u> behavior. What would you expect a <u>professional</u> to do at work? How would he or she dress, behave, and interact?

LESSON 2

A. WORD FAMILIES

Study the five word families below. Then fill in the word form chart. The underlined word forms at the top of the list are the most commonly used forms in academic texts.

demonstrate	ensure	challenge (2X)	outcome	predict
/ˈdɛmənˌstreɪt/	/ɛnˈʃʊr/	/ˈtʃæləndʒ/	/ˈaʊtˌkʌm/	/prɪˈdɪkt/
demonstrable		challenged		predictable
demonstrator		challenger		predictably
demonstration		challenging		prediction
demonstrative				predictability
				unpredictable

Exercise - Word Form Chart

NOUN	VERB	ADJECTIVE	ADVERB
1. 2.	1. demonstrate	1. 2.	
	1. ensure		
1. challenge 2.	1.	1. 2.	
1. outcome			
1. 2.	1. predict	1. 2.	1.

B. READING

The Challenge of Advertising

A major <u>challenge</u> of advertising is having to be creative all of the time. To be a good advertising professional, one has to <u>demonstrate</u> creativity on a daily basis. For example, when Sara went to work for an advertising firm, we <u>predicted</u> that she would excel in her new profession because we knew that she was very artistic. However, being artistic does not <u>ensure</u> success in advertising. Not only do you need to be artistic, but you also have to think quickly and continually produce new ideas in a short amount of time. We never dreamed that the <u>outcome</u> of Sara's career decision would be so disappointing; she quit after her first year on the job.

C. COMPREHENSION CHECK

Exercise 1

Refer to the previous reading and use the context to guess the meanings of the words below. Then match the words to their definitions. Do NOT use a dictionary.

___ 1. challenge   A. something which is difficult but rewarding

___ 2. outcome   B. to secure or guarantee

___ 3. ensure   C. said that something would happen before it happened; foretold

___ 4. predicted   D. to show how something works

___ 5. demonstrate   E. result

Exercise 2

True or False? Write T or F in the blanks provided.

___ 1. Learning a foreign language is a <u>challenging</u> experience.

___ 2. The luxury ship *Titanic* experienced a <u>predicted</u> disaster.

___ 3. One of the <u>outcomes</u> of terrorist threats is heightened security at airports.

___ 4. When teaching pronunciation, a teacher should <u>demonstrate</u> how to make difficult sounds.

___ 5. In order to <u>ensure</u> that we would be on time, we left home thirty minutes after the party began.

D. WORD STUDY
Exercise

Many words have more than one meaning. Consider the various meanings of the word **challenge**.

1. challenge (v) – to ask or dare someone to play a game or sport
2. challenge (v) – to test one's abilities
3. challenge (v) – to question, confront, dispute
4. challenge (n) – an invitation to play a game or sport
5. challenge (n) – a difficult job

Read the sentences below and decide if the meaning is 1, 2, 3, 4, or 5.

____ 1. The geography questions will be a <u>challenge</u> for the younger children in the National Geography contest.

____ 2. In many movies depicting the Middle Ages, enemies often <u>challenge</u> each other to sword fights to settle arguments.

____ 3. The University of North Texas chess team issued a <u>challenge</u> that the Southern Methodist University chess team could not refuse.

____ 4. The student was very argumentative and constantly <u>challenged</u> the teacher's rules in the class.

____ 5 The vocabulary test for this unit will <u>challenge</u> your ability to remember and utilize these words.

E. USING WORDS IN COMMUNICATION
Exercise 1

Imagine that you and your partner have just finished a difficult science class. Discuss your time in the class using the following vocabulary words:
challenge, demonstrate, ensure, outcomes, predicted.

Exercise 2

Repeat and complete the following sentences.

1. I could have <u>predicted</u> that…
2. When students <u>demonstrate</u> at universities…
3. One study technique that <u>ensures</u> academic success is…
4. One of the <u>challenges</u> for a new political leader is to…
5. One of the <u>outcomes</u> of studying at a U.S. university will be…

LESSON 3

A. WORD FAMILIES

Study the five word families below. Then fill in the word form chart. The underlined word forms at the top of the list are the most commonly used forms in academic texts.

alter	despite	series	goal	job
/ˈɔltər/	/dɪˈspaɪt/	/ˈsɪriz/	/goʊl/	/dʒɑb/
alterable				
alteration				
altered				
alternate (3X)*				

* used three times in Word Form Chart

Exercise - Word Form Chart

NOUN	VERB	ADJECTIVE	PREPOSITION
1. 2.	1. alter 2.	1. 2. 3.	
			1. despite
1. series			
1. goal			
1. job			

B. READING

A Seamstress

A seamstress has a challenging <u>job</u>. She must create an article of clothing to fit a particular individual. If she achieves her <u>goal</u> and makes something beautiful or useful, she may be asked to do a <u>series</u> of jobs for one customer. Sometimes, <u>despite</u> doing an excellent job of making an article of clothing, a seamstress may be asked to <u>alter</u> a garment because her customer gained weight, lost weight, or wants to loan the garment to a friend. It's tough being a good seamstress.

C. COMPREHENSION CHECK

Exercise 1

Refer to the previous reading and use the context to guess the meanings of the words below. Then match the words to their definitions. Do NOT use a dictionary.

___ 1. alter	A.	a post of employment; position
___ 2. despite	B.	to change something
___ 3. goal	C.	in spite of; notwithstanding
___ 4. job	D.	a group or a number of related or similar things
___ 5. series	E.	target; what you hope to achieve

Exercise 2

Answer the questions with YES or NO.

_____ 1. Can you <u>alter</u> your own genes?

_____ 2. Do you have to work to reach your <u>goals</u>?

_____ 3. Do you need a <u>job</u> to get money?

_____ 4. Can roses bloom <u>despite</u> a lack of water and sunshine?

_____ 5. Is a <u>series</u> only one thing?

D. WORD STUDY

Exercise

In the English language, certain words are used together regularly and sound correct together. These are called collocations. For example, a common collocation with <u>alternate</u>, one of the words in this unit, is <u>alternate plan</u>. Look at other collocations for other words in this unit. Try to guess the correct answers focusing on the meanings you've learned for the vocabulary words in this unit.

alternate plan	primary goal	job security

Circle the letter of the correct answers for these collocations.

1. In case of rain, what would be a good <u>alternate plan</u> for going to the beach?
   a. having a picnic in the park
   b. going to see a movie
   c. playing tennis outdoors

2. What is the <u>primary goal</u> of most governments?
   a. world domination
   b. to provide for its people's basic needs
   c. religious conversion of the masses

3. When do people have more <u>job security</u>?
   a. during times of economic growth
   b. during a recession
   c. during a depression

E. USING WORDS IN COMMUNICATION
Exercise 1
Answer the following:

1. If you could <u>alter</u> some part of your body, what would you change? Why?

2. Describe some of the <u>goals</u> you have set for yourself.

3. What <u>series</u> of procedures did you have to follow to apply to school?

4. If you could have any <u>job</u> at all, what job would you most like to have?

5. Complete this thought. "I love my boyfriend/girlfriend/sister/brother <u>despite</u>...."

Exercise 2
Role Play - With a partner, create a story using the following words: **alter, despite, goal, job, series.** Tell the story to another pair of students.

LESSON 4

A. WORD FAMILIES

Study the five word families below. Then fill in the word form chart. The underlined word forms at the top of the list are the most commonly used forms in academic texts.

annual (2X)	illustrate	imply	mental	target (2X)
/ˈænyuəl/	/ˈɪləˌstreɪt/	/ɪmˈplaɪ/	/ˈmɛntl/	/ˈtɑrgɪt/
annually	illustrated	implication	mentality	targeted
	illustration		mentally	
	illustrative			

Exercise - Word Form Chart

NOUN	VERB	ADJECTIVE	ADVERB
1.		1. annual	1.
1.	1. illustrate	1. 2.	
1.	1. imply		
1.		1. mental	1.
1. target	1.	1.	

B. READING

Men's Favorite Magazine

Every year *Sports Illustrated* publishes its annual swimsuit edition. The magazine's name is *Sports Illustrated*, which implies that there will be pictures of sporting events like baseball and basketball. However, the purpose of the annual swimsuit edition, which features beautiful young women in skimpy bikinis, is to increase sales by attracting more readers from the magazine's target market, which consists of men between the ages of thirteen and forty-five. Executives at the magazine hope that their readers will make a mental connection between buying their magazine and meeting beautiful young women. Thus, they increase their sales each year.

C. COMPREHENSION CHECK
Exercise 1
Refer to the previous reading and use the context to guess the meanings of the words below. Then match the words to their definitions. Do NOT use a dictionary.

____ 1. annual	A. accompanied by pictures or examples
____ 2. illustrated	B. goal
____ 3. implies	C. having to do with the mind
____ 4. mental	D. seems to indicate; hints; suggests
____ 5. target	E. happening once a year

Exercise 2
Choose the word that is different in meaning.

1. target	aim	objective	miss
2. annual	weekly	yearly	twelve-monthly
3. illustrated	shown	counted	exemplified
4. mental	physical	cerebral	psychological
5. imply	mean	count	suggest

D. WORD STUDY
Exercise
Choose the correct word form for each blank.

1. My dictionary is an _____ version. My partner's is not.
   a. illustration   b. illustrated   c. illustrate

2. His psychiatrist declared him _____ unstable.
   a. mental   b. mentality   c. mentally

3. We don't throw darts at animals. Instead, we throw them at _____.
   a. target   b. targeted   c. targets

4. His lack of faith in God was _____ in his writing.
   a. implies   b. imply   c. implied

5. That journal is published _____.
   a. annual   b. annually

E. USING WORDS IN COMMUNICATION
Exercise

With a partner, discuss the following:

1. What are some things that you do <u>annually</u>?

2. Have you ever <u>illustrated</u> anything? If so, what did you <u>illustrate</u>?

3. Describe a <u>mental</u> problem that you know about. Do you know anybody who suffers from this <u>mental</u> problem?

4. Do you think that a person's name <u>implies</u> something about his personality? Why or why not?

5. Think of some sports which have <u>targets</u>. Name as many of them as you can.

Review

The crossword puzzle below contains all 20 words from Unit 1. Solve the puzzle by filling in the blanks to complete the sentences on the next page.

ACROSS

3. Teaching is not just a _____ . It's a profession.
4. Sportscasters _____ that the Yankees would win the World Series again, but they were wrong.
8. I didn't make just one mistake. I made a whole _____ of them!
9. Superman has amazing physical powers, but he doesn't have any impressive _____ powers.
11. Doctors and lawyers are _____ people. They are well-respected for what they do.
15. I asked her to _____ the method, but she wouldn't show me what to do.
18. Zelda bought a dress that is too big. She hired a seamstress to _____ her dress.
19. We wanted to _____ our baby's good health, so we fed her the best vitamins and food that we could afford.

DOWN

1. _____ are difficult to predict, especially when many people are involved.
2. The _____ of his misery is his bad childhood.
5. I like mathematics because it's difficult but fun. It's a _____ for me.
6. My children's book is being _____ by my best friend, the artist.
7. I love him _____ his faults.
10. I wish people wouldn't _____ blondes as dumb airheads.
12. The sun is the Earth's main source of _____ .
13. His sad eyes _____ that he was unhappy.
14. Every year we have our _____ bazaar.
16. To get a good job is his _____ in life.
17. I'm not a very good shot. I rarely hit the _____ .
20. His sister is suffering from too much _____ . Between her long working hours, her three children, and her demanding husband, she has too many responsibilities.

UNIT 2

WORDS

academic	contrast	framework	occupational
approximate	cycle	generation	phase
attitude	debate	immigration	publish
circumstance	deduction	internal	prior
compensation	error	obvious	validity

READINGS

A Professor's Challenge
Coming to America
The Internal Revenue Service
Erikson's Phases of Life

STRATEGIES AND SKILLS

Word Forms
- Word family charts
- Word form selection

Comprehension Check
- Matching definitions
- Understanding and using words in context
- Identifying synonyms

Word Expansion
- Collocations
- Multiple meanings

Interactive Speaking Practice
- Sentence completion
- Storytelling
- Listing
- Role play

ACADEMIC WORD POWER

LESSON 1

A. WORD FAMILIES

Study the five word families below. Then fill in the word form chart. The underlined word forms at the top of the list are the most commonly used forms in academic texts.

academic (2X)	debate (2X)	validity	publish	occupational
/ˌækəˈdɛmɪk/	/dɪˈbeɪt/	/vəˈlɪdəti/	/ˈpʌblɪʃ/	/ˌɑkyəˈpeɪʃənəl/
academia	debatable	valid	published	occupation
academy		validate	publisher	
academically		validation		
		invalidate		

Exercise - Word Form Chart

NOUN	VERB	ADJECTIVE	ADVERB
1. 2. 3.		1. academic	1.
1. debate	1.	1.	
1. validity 2.	1. 2.	1.	
1.	1. publish	1.	
1.		1. occupational	

B. READING

A Professor's Challenge

One of the challenges of a professor's life is meeting the demands of academia. Not only does a professor teach classes, but she also must conduct research and publish articles in academic journals. If a professor's research is not published on a regular basis, she may not get to keep her job. There is a long-standing debate in universities about this pressure to "publish or perish." Some argue that it is merely an occupational requirement, while others maintain that the pressure to publish is unrealistic because a professor's primary role is to teach students. Many people question the validity of an expectation that shifts a professor's energy away from her students and toward writing and research.

C. COMPREHENSION CHECK

Exercise 1

Refer to the reading above and use the context to guess the meaning of the words below. Then match the words to their definitions. Do NOT use a dictionary.

___ 1. academic   A. an argument between two opposing sides

___ 2. debate   B. featured in a journal, newspaper, or book

___ 3. validity   C. state of being correct or authoritative

___ 4. published   D. having to do with a school, especially higher education

___ 5. occupational   E. caused by the conditions of a particular job

Exercise 2

True or False? Write T or F in the blanks provided.

___ 1. Teaching and learning are not <u>academic</u> concerns.

___ 2. There is much <u>debate</u> about the issue of abortion.

___ 3. Many computer manuals are originally <u>published</u> in English.

___ 4. Falling beams and blocks are an <u>occupational</u> hazard for construction workers.

___ 5. One should question the <u>validity</u> of so-called scientific findings that go against common sense.

D. WORD STUDY

Exercise 1

These are some common collocations for words in this unit.

academic freedom	scientific validity	occupational hazard
political debate	published report	

Circle the letter of the correct answers for these collocations.

1. Which of the following is an example of <u>academic freedom</u>?
   a. Students and teachers are allowed to wear whatever they want.
   b. A professor publishes an article in the local paper which does not reflect the views of the university, but he is not fired.
   c. A student turns in a report which he borrows from friend.

2. Which of the following issues would **not** cause <u>political debate</u>?
   a. a national budget (how to spend a nation's money)
   b. freedom to carry a gun
   c. studying in high school

3. How can <u>scientific validity</u> be tested?
   a. by doing experiments
   b. by consulting an astrological chart
   c. by speaking to experts

4. Which of the following is a <u>published report</u>?
   a. an oral report on the state of the Union
   b. an article in *Nature* magazine
   c. a paper for a university-level chemistry course

5. Which of the following is an <u>occupational hazard</u> of professional boxing?
   a. bruises
   b. falling rocks
   c. paper cuts

Exercise 2
Choose the correct word form for each blank.

1. My father is a college professor, so he is an _____.
   a. academy   b. academic   c. academia

2. I always look forward to the presidential _____.
   a. debated   b. debatable   c. debates

3. After a student graduates from his university, his student identification card is no longer _____.
   a. valid   b. validating   c. validation

4. The Houghton Mifflin company is a well-known example of a _____ of textbooks.
   a. publish   b. publisher   c. publishing

5. A student must choose his or her _____ carefully because she will probably be doing it every day for a long time.
   a. occupant   b. occupancy   c. occupation

E. USING WORDS IN COMMUNICATION
Exercise 1
Repeat and complete the following sentences.

1. If I could choose to study at any <u>academy</u> of higher learning, I would choose…
2. An issue which is currently under <u>debate</u> internationally is…
3. A <u>valid</u> complaint of international students is…
4. I would like to <u>publish</u>…
5. When I daydream in class, my mind is <u>occupied</u> by thoughts of …

Exercise 2
First, read through the five words: **academic, debate, validity, published, occupational**. With a partner, make up a paragraph or story that includes all the words. Then read the paragraph or story to the class. Be creative!

LESSON 2

A. WORD FAMILIES

Study the five word families below. Then fill in the word form chart. The underlined word forms at the top of the list are the most commonly used forms in academic texts.

circumstance	prior	attitude	cycle (2X)	immigration
/'sɜrkəmˌstæns/	/'praɪər/	/'ætəˌtud/	/'saɪkəl/	/ˌɪmə'greɪʃən/
	priority		cyclic	immigrate
			cyclical	immigrant

Exercise - Word Form Chart

NOUN	VERB	ADJECTIVE	ADVERB
1. circumstance			
1.		1. prior	
1. attitude			
1. cycle	1.	1. 2.	
1. immigration 2.	1.		

B. READING

Coming to America

The United States of America is a land of immigrants. Spanish, French, and English immigrants who came here <u>prior</u> to 1776 settled the land. Despite the fact that almost all U.S. citizens are descended from immigrants, <u>attitudes</u> toward immigrants have changed depending on <u>circumstances</u>. For example, during the late nineteenth century when the United States became more industrialized, many immigrants came here from Southern and Eastern Europe. Since the economy was growing and their labor was necessary, they were welcomed by the older immigrants. However, the <u>cycle</u> of <u>immigration</u> is such that one group moves up the social ladder as it develops its skills and place in society, while another group moves in and occupies the bottom of the ladder, taking the less desirable jobs, such as cleaning or dangerous work. U.S. citizens' attitudes toward these new immigrants change over time; at first they usually dislike the people but welcome their labor, but eventually they grow to like the people as well.

C. COMPREHENSION CHECK
Exercise 1
Refer to the previous reading and use the context to guess the meaning of the words below. Then match the words to their definitions. Do NOT use a dictionary.

___ 1. attitudes

___ 2. circumstances

___ 3. cycle

___ 4. immigration

___ 5. prior

A. feelings about a person or thing

B. the act of coming to live in a foreign country

C. conditions that accompany, determine, or modify a fact or event

D. preceding in time or order; earlier

E. a sequence of events that happen again and again in the same order

Exercise 2
True or False? Write T or F in the blanks provided.

___ 1. Some people's attitudes toward immigration are negative.

___ 2. Circumstances surrounding a person's death can be mysterious.

___ 3. Prior to the year 1800, there were no portable computers.

___ 4. The cycle of poverty is unbreakable as poverty always repeats itself in the next generation.

___ 5. Immigration to a new country requires a big commitment.

D. WORD STUDY
Exercise
Most words have more than one meaning. Consider the various meanings of the word **cycle.**

---

1. cycle (v) - to ride or travel by bicycle or motorcycle

2. cycle (v) - to move in cycles

3. cycle (n) - a bicycle, motorcycle, tricycle, or the like

4. cycle (n) - a recurring series of events

Use either 1, 2, 3, or 4 to note which meaning is used in each sentence.

___ 1. I love the way seasons cycle through the year.

___ 2. It's a beautiful day. Let's cycle through the park!

___ 3. His cycle is blue, but mine is silver.

___ 4. In tropical countries, the weather cycle generally consists of wet seasons followed by dry seasons.

E. USING WORDS IN COMMUNICATION
Exercise 1

1. List 3 countries that benefit from <u>immigration</u>.

2. List 3 <u>circumstances</u> that are beyond your control.

3. List 3 parts of the life <u>cycle.</u> (*Hint* - The first part is birth.)

4. List 3 modes of transportation which existed <u>prior</u> to the invention of the airplane.

5. List 3 <u>attitudes</u> that bother or upset you.

Exercise 2
Discuss the following with a partner.

1. Agree or disagree with this statement: <u>Immigration</u> is good for the U.S. but bad for other countries.

2. I would marry a man or woman I didn't know very well only under the following <u>circumstances.</u> (Give your opinion.)

3. Describe the weather <u>cycle</u> where you live.

4. Think back to right before you took your last trip. Describe the week <u>prior</u> to your departure.

5. What is your <u>attitude</u> about reality shows on TV?

LESSON 3

A. WORD FAMILIES
Study the five word families below. Then fill in the word form chart. The underlined word forms at the top of the list are the most commonly used forms in academic texts.

compensation	contrast (2x)	obvious	internal	error
/ˌkɑmpənˈseɪʃən/	/ˈkɑnˌtræst/	/ˈɑbvɪəs/	/ɪnˈtɜrnəl/	/ˈɛrər/
compensate	contrastive	obviously	internalize	erroneous
compensatory			internally	erroneously

Exercise - Word Form Chart

NOUN	VERB	ADJECTIVE	ADVERB
1. compensation	1.	1.	
1.	1. contrast	1.	
		1. obvious	1.
	1.	1. internal	1.
1. error		1.	1.

B. READING

The Internal Revenue Service

There is a federal agency which people in the U.S. love to hate. It's called the <u>Internal Revenue Service</u> (IRS). Its responsibility is to collect federal income tax from all people who earn income in the U.S. It must keep track of each worker's pay and charge tax according to how much total <u>compensation</u> he or she earns in a year. Because there are so many people paying taxes in America, it is easy to make <u>errors</u>. It is <u>obvious</u> that not every penny that every person earns can be easily accounted for. As a result, problems frequently arise when people pay too much tax or, in <u>contrast</u>, pay too little.

C. COMPREHENSION CHECK
Exercise 1
Refer to the reading above and use the context to guess the meaning of the words below. Then match the words to their definitions. Do NOT use a dictionary.

___ 1. compensation   A. easy to see
___ 2. contrast   B. to compare in order to show difference
___ 3. errors   C. inside of someone or something
___ 4. internal   D. mistakes
___ 5. obvious   E. something given or received as an equivalent for services, debt, loss, or injury

Exercise 2
Which word does not belong?

1. payment	compensation	salary	bill
2. contrast	distinction	unalike	same
3. internal	within	outdoors	inside
4. error	achievement	fault	mistake
5. obvious	apparent	clear	mysterious

D. WORD STUDY
Exercise 1
Choose the correct word form for each blank.

1. It was a _____ gesture; he owed me for all the favors I had done for him in the past.

   a. compensate   b. compensation   c. compensatory

2. The professor was very good at comparing businesses, but his _____ analysis was weak.

   a. contrast   b. contrastive   c. contrasted

3. People in my family tend to _____ all our problems.

   a. internal   b. internally   c. internalize

4. He made an _____ assumption; the girls were not going to give up the fight as easily as he had thought.

   a. error   b. erroneous   c. erroneously

5. The consequence of failing to complete the course requirements is _____. You will receive a failing grade.

   a. obvious   b. obviously

Exercise 2

These are some common collocations for words in this unit.

due compensation	internal conflict	stark contrast
erroneous assumption	obvious disparity	

Circle the letter of the correct answers for these collocations.

1. What is <u>due compensation</u> for the survivor of an auto accident that can be blamed on the vehicle's faulty design?

   a. payment of hospital bills and some amount of money for pain and suffering

   b. a vacation in Hawaii

   c. absolutely nothing

2. Which of the following is an example of an <u>internal conflict</u>?

   a. the American Revolution

   b. Sierra Leone's civil war

   c. World War II

3. What would be a <u>stark contrast</u> to a life of luxury?

   a. a life of severe poverty

   b. a middle-class existence

   c. a life of solitude

4. When there is an <u>obvious disparity</u> in income among a country's citizens, what conditions does one expect to find?

   a. all the citizens have nice cars and houses

   b. some people live in beautiful mansions, while others live in ugly shacks

   c. police are well-paid, as are garbage collectors

5. Which of the following is an example of an <u>erroneous assumption</u>?

   a. sometimes leaders make mistakes

   b. most students go to school to learn

   c. all educated people are kind

E. USING WORDS IN COMMUNICATION
Exercise 1
Answer the following:

1. What do you think is fair <u>compensation</u> for a day's work as a garbage collector?

2. <u>Contrast</u> your previous English class to this class.

3. What's the worst <u>error</u> you have ever made?

4. What are the <u>obvious</u> concerns of parents?

5. Can you name five <u>internal</u> organs? What are they?

Exercise 2
Role Play - You and your partner are owners of a big firm. Employees have been complaining about their low pay and your high pay. With your partner, write a short speech which will address the issue at hand. The speech will be given tomorrow at a general assembly. (Use these words: **compensation, contrast, error, internal, obvious**.)

LESSON 4

A. WORD FAMILIES

Study the five word families below. Then fill in the word form chart. The underlined word forms at the top of the list are the most commonly used forms in academic texts.

<u>phase</u> (2X)
/feɪz/

<u>generation</u>
/ˌdʒɛnəˈreɪʃən/

<u>framework</u>
/ˈfreɪmˌwɜrk/

<u>deduction</u>
/dɪˈdʌkʃən/
deduce

<u>approximate</u> (2X)
/əˈprɑksəˌmeɪt/
approximately
approximation

Exercise - Word Form Chart

NOUN	VERB	ADJECTIVE	ADVERB
1. phase	1.		
1. generation			
1. framework			
1. deduction	1.		
1.	1. approximate	1.	1.

B. READING

Erikson's Phases of Life

Every twenty years a new <u>generation</u> reaches adulthood. Adulthood is one of the many <u>phases</u> that humans go through in their lives. Psychologists as well as philosophers have given us a <u>framework</u> for thinking about life's phases and the resulting differences between the generations. A famous psychologist named Erik Erikson described the various phases of life. He <u>approximated</u> that in the average life span of seventy years, an individual goes through six stages: infancy, childhood, adolescence, early adulthood, adulthood, and old age. Of course, anyone could have arrived at his conclusion by the process of <u>deduction</u>, but Erikson gets credit for identifying and describing these distinct phases of life.

C. COMPREHENSION CHECK
Exercise 1
Refer to the previous reading and use the context to guess the meaning of the words below.
Then match the words to their definitions. Do NOT use a dictionary.

___	1. approximated	A.	stages in a process of development
___	2. generation	B.	estimated
___	3. framework	C.	a group of people of about the same age
___	4. phases	D.	an organization of ideas
___	5. deduction	E.	reaching a conclusion by reasoning from the general to the specific

Exercise 2
Fill in the blank using the appropriate vocabulary word.

1. The _____ for our proposal is found in this report.
2. College freshmen go through an initial _____ of orientation in which they learn their way around the university.
3. My grandparents' _____ suffered a lot more than my own.
4. Sherlock Holmes was a brilliant investigator who skillfully used the processes of induction and _____ to arrive at his solutions to mysteries.
5. Because the referee did not see exactly where the ball went out of bounds, he _____ the site, and play resumed from that area.

D. WORD STUDY
Exercise
Many words in English commonly collocate with certain prepositions. Often, the meanings of the words are changed slightly depending on the preposition with which they are used. Study the following examples with the word **phase**.

> 1. phase in – to put or come into use gradually
>
> 2. phase out – to bring or come to an end gradually; to ease out of service
>
> 3. phase down – to reduce or diminish by gradual stages

Fill in the blanks using the appropriate phrasal verb. Change verb tense or voice if necessary.

1. We did not want to shock our customers with sudden changes to our product line, so we slowly _____ them _____.
2. The Cadillac used to be a very big car, but over the years, it has been _____ _____.
3. As DVD players become more popular, VCRs are being _____ _____.

E. USING WORDS IN COMMUNICATION
Exercise 1
With a partner, discuss the following:

1. Describe your <u>generation</u>. How does it differ from your parents' <u>generation</u>?

2. What are some <u>phases</u> that all babies go through?

3. Using the process of <u>deduction</u>, what can you infer about one of your classmates? (Remember to go from the general to the specific.)

Exercise 2
Repeat and complete the following sentences. Fill in the blanks.

1. I am <u>approximately</u> _____ feet (or meters) tall and weigh <u>approximately</u> _____ pounds (or kilograms).

2. _____ should be <u>phased</u> out of existence.

3. My grandparents' <u>generation</u> is very ...

4. From your appearance, I can <u>deduce</u>...

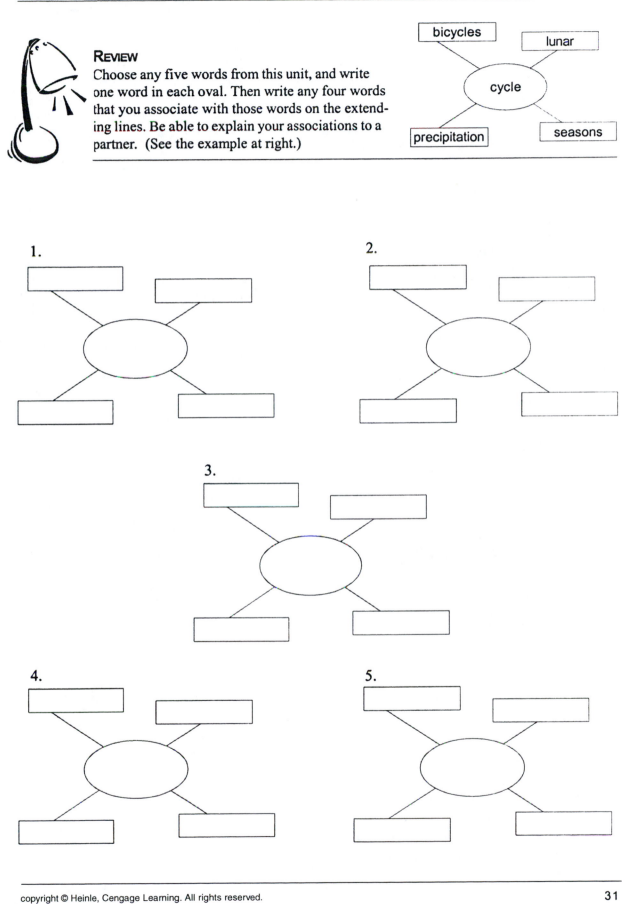

REVIEW

Choose any five words from this unit, and write one word in each oval. Then write any four words that you associate with those words on the extending lines. Be able to explain your associations to a partner. (See the example at right.)

bicycles • lunar • cycle • precipitation • seasons

1.

2.

3.

4.

5.

UNIT 3

WORDS

alternative	emerge	license	reject
constant	external	medical	style
contribution	fundamental	modify	sum
corresponding	image	option	sustainable
dominant	investigation	project	transition

READINGS

The Development Issue
Fashion
Licensing Agencies
The Trials of Orenthal James Simpson

STRATEGIES AND SKILLS

Word Forms
- Word family charts
- Word form selection

Comprehension Check
- Matching definitions
- Recognizing words in context
- Identifying synonyms

Word Expansion
- Collocations
- Multiple meanings
- Suffixes

Interactive Speaking Practice
- Sentence completion
- Role Play
- Listing
- Associations

ACADEMIC WORD POWER

LESSON 1

A. WORD FAMILIES

Study the five word families below. Then fill in the word form chart. The underlined word forms at the top of the list are the most commonly used forms in academic texts.

emerge	project (2X)	reject (2X)	medical	sustainable
/ɪˈmɜrdʒ/	/ˈprɑˌdʒɛkt/	/rɪˈdʒɛkt/	/ˈmɛdɪkəl/	/səˈsteɪnəbəl/
emergence	projected	rejected	medically	sustain
emergent	projection	rejection	medicine	sustainability
emerging			medicate	sustained
				sustenance
				unsustainable

Exercise - Word Form Chart

NOUN	VERB	ADJECTIVE	ADVERB
1.	1. emerge	1. 2.	
1. project 2.	1.	1.	
1. 2.	1. reject	1.	
1.	1.	1. medical	1.
1. 2.	1.	1. sustainable 2. 3.	

B. READING

The Development Issue

One of the greatest challenges in international relations is the issue of development. For the last fifty years, highly industrialized countries, such as the United States and Great Britain, have been sending experts to less developed countries to help needy countries develop their resources. Projects include building roads, training medical personnel, planting trees, training teachers, and improving agricultural yields. The intentions of development agents are basically good. However, a serious problem has emerged. Many projects are not sustainable. That is, once the experts leave, the local people cannot keep the projects running by themselves. As a result, large development projects that require experts from highly developed nations are now routinely rejected, while small, sustainable projects are favored.

C. COMPREHENSION CHECK

Exercise 1

Refer to the reading above and use the context to guess the meanings of the words below. Then match the words to their definitions. Do NOT use a dictionary.

___ 1. emerged	A. became known or important
___ 2. projects	B. related to medicine
___ 3. rejected	C. able to be kept in existence or maintained
___ 4. medical	D. specific tasks
___ 5. sustainable	E. refused because not good enough

Exercise 2

True or False? Write T or F in the blanks provided.

___ 1. When you are sick, you should go to the doctor for a <u>medical</u> consultation.
___ 2. 100 miles per hour is a <u>sustainable</u> speed on most highways.
___ 3. Building a house is a <u>project</u> that can be finished in less than a day.
___ 4. In the 1980's and 1990's several Asian economies <u>emerged</u> onto the world stage.
___ 5. Sometimes teenagers <u>reject</u> their parents' advice and prefer to listen to their peers instead.

D. WORD STUDY

Exercise 1

These are some common collocations for words in this unit.

sustainable development	medical necessity	
emergent democracy	total rejection	research project

Circle the letter of the correct answers for these collocations.

1. Which of the following is an example of a <u>total rejection</u>?
   a. a publishing company sends a manuscript back to the author for revision before publication
   b. a corporation sends a job applicant a letter saying he/she is not qualified
   c. a young woman sometimes goes out with a young man when he invites her, but sometimes she does not

2. Which of the following procedures is **not** a <u>medical necessity</u>?
   a. removal of cancerous lesions or lumps
   b. surgery to clear a blocked artery
   c. eye surgery to correct nearsightedness

3. Identify the project which exemplifies <u>sustainable development</u>.
   a. Villagers are given tools and seeds and told to plant a new crop that can be sold for cash. The crop will exhaust the soil's fertility after two growing seasons.
   b. Village women are allowed to buy sewing machines at low prices with small low-interest loans. Using the machines, the women create their own small businesses as seamstresses.
   c. Developers build a recreation center with basketball hoops and ping-pong tables. All building materials are imported, and the villagers prefer soccer and running.

4. Which of the following is an important <u>research project</u>?
    a. studying the ability of bacteria to survive on Pluto
    b. searching for a vaccine for AIDS or cancer
    c. investigating the whereabouts of Elvis Presley

5. What characteristics does an <u>emergent democracy</u> possess?
    a. anarchy, economic freefall, revolutionaries
    b. mature and experienced government, capitalistic tendencies, wealth
    c. social stability, new leadership, representation of all people

Exercise 2 - Word Forms
Choose the correct word form for each blank.

1. Sam does not know how much money he will make next year. Two hundred thousand dollars is just a _____.
   a. project   b. projected   c. projection

2. Both men and women hate to be _____.
   a. rejection   b. rejected   c. reject

3. His insurance company claimed that his procedure was not _____ necessary. As a result, they refused to pay his bill.
   a. medically   b. medical   c. medic

4. In Eastern countries, rice is the staple crop. On the other hand, in Western countries, bread is the primary form of _____.
   a. sustainability   b. sustain   c. sustenance

5. In springtime, every kind of natural life seems to _____. Flowers bloom, babies are born, and bears awake from their long winter naps.
   a. emerged   b. emerge   c. emerging

E. USING WORDS IN COMMUNICATION
Exercise 1
Repeat and complete the following sentences:

1. An <u>unsustainable</u> job is…
2. A time I felt <u>rejected</u> was when…
3. Several <u>projects</u> I need to do in my room/apartment are…
4. A problem that has <u>emerged</u> in the last few weeks is…
5. I would/wouldn't like to be a <u>medical</u> student because…

Exercise 2
Role Play - With a partner, perform a role play between a parent and a child. Using the vocabulary words in this lesson, discuss the child's plan to apply to medical school. Use these words:

medical   rejected   sustainable   emerged   project

LESSON 2

A. WORD FAMILIES

Study the five word families below. Then fill in the word form chart. The underlined word forms at the top of the list are the most commonly used forms in academic texts.

alternative (2X)	fundamental	style (2X)	image	dominant
/ɔl'tɜrnətɪv/	/ˌfʌndə'mɛntəl/	/staɪl/	/'ɪmɪdʒ/	/'dɑmənənt/
alternatively	fundamentally	stylish	imagery	dominate
		stylized		dominance
				dominating
				domination

Exercise 1 - Word Form Chart

NOUN	VERB	ADJECTIVE	ADVERB
1.		1. alternative	1.
		1. fundamental	1.
1. style	1.	1. 2.	
1. image 2.			
1. 2.	1.	1. dominant 2.	

B. READING

Fashion

Fashion is all about creating and projecting an <u>image</u>. People who follow the current fashions know what <u>styles</u> of clothing and hairstyle are popular. Many people wear these fashions because doing so is <u>fundamental</u> to acceptance in social groups. However, not everybody wants to be a part of the <u>dominant</u> social group, the one that sets the trends and generally has the most followers. Some fashion buffs choose an <u>alternative</u> route. They either find a fashion that suits their own personal taste and stick with it, or they dress in the fashion of a less popular group and conform to its ideas about what is attractive. Whichever way people choose to express themselves, they still use fashion to project an image.

C. COMPREHENSION CHECK
Exercise 1
Refer to the reading above and use the context to guess the meanings of the words below. Then match the words to their definitions. Do NOT use a dictionary.

___ 1. alternative

A. holding the most important position or greatest influence

___ 2. fundamental

B. different

___ 3. styles

C. one's appearance to others

___ 4. image

D. basic, primary

___ 5. dominant

E. particular ways that things are done

Exercise 2
Which word does not belong?

1. alternative	option	substitute	same
2. dominant	powerful	small	major
3. image	hurt	appearance	look
4. styles	calendars	approaches	methods
5. fundamental	essential	first	unimportant

D. WORD STUDY
Exercise 1
Some words have more than one meaning. Consider the various meanings of the word **image**.

1. image (n) - a mental picture of someone or something
2. image (n) - picture, copy
3. image (n) - one's appearance to others, reputation

Use either 1, 2, or 3 to note which meaning is used in each sentence.

___ 1. Modern U.S. politicians are obsessed with image.

___ 2. I have an image of you when you were ten years old, standing in the snow and looking up at the sky. That's how I always think of you.

___ 3. The boss said he needed that image yesterday for a presentation he did for the board of directors.

___ 4. Even for a man who tried to live simply like Mohatma Gandhi, image was crucial to his success.

Exercise 2
Choose the correct word form for each blank.

1. During World War II, men had two _____. They could either join the armed forces or be drafted.
   a. alternative   b. alternatively   c. alternatives

2. His theory was _____ flawed because he failed to take all the variables into account.
   a. fundamental   b. fundamentally

3. Much research has focused on individual learning _____.
   a. styles   b. styling   c. stylish

4. Use of _____ is one of the many conventions of poetry.
   a. image   b. imagery   c. images

5. There is one student in our class who tries to _____ every class discussion.
   a. dominant   b. dominance   c. dominate

E. USING WORDS IN COMMUNICATION
Exercise 1

1. List 3 <u>alternatives</u> to war.
2. List 3 <u>fundamental</u> values that you live by.
3. List 3 <u>styles</u> of dress that appeal to you.
4. List 3 <u>images</u> that come to mind when you think of Christmas.
5. List 3 issues which currently <u>dominate</u> the media.

Exercise 2
Discuss the following.

1. Agree or disagree with this statement: Teaching <u>styles</u> are important to the learning process. (Explain your opinion.)

2. Some people argue that <u>image</u> is more important than a politician's beliefs. Do you agree or disagree?

3. The <u>dominant</u> ethnic group in the United States is of Western European descent. What do you think is the second most <u>dominant</u> ethnic group?

4. A <u>fundamental</u> assumption in the United States is that everyone wants to get ahead (i.e., get more than they have). How do you feel about this assumption?

5. Describe an <u>alternative</u> to cars as a mode of transportation.

LESSON 3

A. WORD FAMILIES

Study the five word families below. Then fill in the word form chart. The underlined word forms at the top of the list are the most commonly used forms in academic texts.

contribution	external	license (2X)	option	sum
/ˌkɑntrəˈbyuʃən/	/ɪkˈstɜrnəl/	/ˈlaɪsəns/	/ˈɑpʃən/	/sʌm/
contribute	externalize	licensed	optional	summation
contributor	externally	licensing		

Exercise - Word Form Chart

NOUN	VERB	ADJECTIVE	ADVERB
1. contribution 2.	1.		
	1.	1. external	1.
1. license	1.	1. 2.	
1. option		1.	
1. sum 2.			

B. READING

Licensing Agencies

In order to do many things in the United States, a <u>license</u> is required. For example, in order to own a gun or drive a car, one must acquire a license. Without a license, your only <u>options</u> are to do these things illegally or not at all. As a result, the <u>contribution</u> that licensing agencies make to society is of great importance to us all. It is not possible to allow private <u>external</u> agencies to license such things as the ability to drive a car or own a gun. Only internal state or federal agencies have that authority. In <u>sum</u>, the work that licensing agencies do is of vital importance to the welfare of society.

C. COMPREHENSION CHECK
Exercise 1
Refer to the reading above and use the context to guess the meanings of the words below. Then match the words to their definitions. Do NOT use a dictionary.

___ 1. contribution	A. choices
___ 2. external	B. the totality of something
___ 3. license	C. outside of someone or something
___ 4. options	D. a permit given by an official body
___ 5. sum	E. positive or helpful participation

Exercise 2
True or False? Write T or F on the line.

___ 1. A <u>license</u> is necessary to have a child.

___ 2. If you want to attend university, you have many <u>options</u>.

___ 3. The Japanese have made important <u>contributions</u> to technology.

___ 4. The <u>sum</u> of four and five is ten.

___ 5. The environment is our <u>external</u> world.

D. WORD STUDY
Exercise
These are some common collocations for words in this unit.

licensed physician	external affairs	payment options
generous contribution	sum total	

Circle the letter of the correct answers for these collocations.

1. Which of the following would be a <u>generous contribution</u> to an elementary school?
   a. ten dollars
   b. a vacation in Hawaii
   c. a donation of land for a new playground

2. What is the <u>sum total</u> of 35,678 and 908,765?
   a. 13,443
   b. 944,443
   c. 94,443

3. What are some valid <u>payment options</u> for the purchase of a new car?
   a. $1000 down payment + 60 months of financing at 0.9% interest
   b. trading a mule and two cows for the car
   c. free food for the car salesman for two years in exchange for the new car

4. Some of the <u>external affairs</u> which are of concern to the United States are:
   a. unemployment benefits and inflation of the U.S. dollar
   b. tariffs in South America and currency fluctuations in Asia
   c. homeland security and the U.S. National Guard

5. Which of the following is an example of a <u>licensed physician</u> in the United States?
   a. a pharmacist
   b. an acupuncturist
   c. a general practitioner of medicine

E. USING WORDS IN COMMUNICATION
Exercise 1
Answer the following:

1. What is the greatest <u>contribution</u> you have made to your family so far?

2. What are some <u>external</u> pressures that influence your life?

3. Do you have a <u>license</u> to do something? What is it for? How did you get it?

4. What are some <u>options</u> you will have after graduation?

5. What <u>sum</u> do you pay each month for living expenses?

Exercise 2
On a sheet of paper, make a list of three to five words you associate with each of the vocabulary words from this lesson, cut up the lists, and see if your partner can put the lists back together again. For example, you might associate **external** with its antonym **internal**. Put it on your list, and see if your partner puts it under the same keyword you did.

| contribution | external | license | option | sum |

LESSON 4

A. WORD FAMILIES

Study the five word families below. Then fill in the word form chart. The underlined word forms at the top of the list are the most commonly used forms in academic texts.

constant (2X)	corresponding	investigation	modify	transition
/ˈkɑnstənt/	/ˌkɔrəˈspɑndɪŋ/	/ɪnˌvɛstəˈgeɪʃən/	/ˈmɑdəˌfaɪ/	/trænˈzɪʃən/
constancy	correspond	investigate	modified	transit (2X)
constantly	correspondence	investigative	modification	transitory
inconstancy	correspondingly	investigator	unmodified	transitional

Exercise - Word Form Chart

NOUN	VERB	ADJECTIVE	ADVERB
1. 2. 3.		1. constant	1.
1.	1.	1. corresponding	1.
1. investigation 2.	1.	1.	
1.	1. modify	1. 2.	
1. transition 2.	1.	1. 2.	

B. READING

The Trials of Orenthal James Simpson

In 1993, the United States was shocked at the live-action car chase of the famous football player O.J. Simpson, who was accused of murdering his ex-wife and her boyfriend. At first, it seemed that he would confess to the murders, but in a short time, he modified his position, claiming to be innocent. A long investigation followed in which the media made constant reports related the progress of the L.A. police department's search for evidence. With no other suspects in the case, it seemed as though the football star would be found guilty, but a jury declared him not guilty. The corresponding outcry could be heard around the world. In spite of the jury's decision, Simpson's peers, wealthy professionals and celebrities who live in the wealthy suburbs of L.A., treated him as though he were guilty. His world was changed forever. It took months for him to make the transition from a highly respected superstar advertising rental cars on TV to a widely scorned celebrity who had fallen from grace. Today, he struggles to pay his enormous bills and keep custody of his children.

C. COMPREHENSION CHECK

Exercise 1

Refer to the previous reading and use the context to guess the meanings of the words below. Then match the words to their definitions. Do NOT use a dictionary.

___ 1. constant   A. relating to, matching

___ 2. corresponding   B. happening all the time, continuous

___ 3. investigation   C. the change from one condition to another

___ 4. modified   D. a search for facts and information

___ 5. transition   E. changed

Exercise 2

Which word does not belong?

1. constant	always	never	continually
2. corresponding	living	related	agreeing
3. investigation	inspection	excitement	exploration
4. modified	concluded	altered	adapted
5. transition	dislike	change	shift

D. WORD STUDY
Exercise 1
These are some common collocations for words in this unit.

constant reminder	special correspondent	investigative reporter
modified version	violent transition	

Circle the letter of the correct answers for these collocations.

1. Which of the following would be a <u>constant reminder</u> of a politician's contribution to an area?
    a. a building with the politician's family name on it
    b. biannual advertisements in the local newspaper
    c. a smoke message printed in the sky by an airplane

2. What would a <u>special correspondent</u> to a magazine do?
    a. buy three yearly subscriptions to the magazine
    b. create advertisements for each issue
    c. occasionally contribute articles expressing her opinions

3. Which of the following is a <u>modified version</u> of a bicycle?
    a. a car
    b. a moped
    c. a jet airliner

4. Which of the following is an example of a <u>violent transition</u> of governments?
    a. the change from British to Chinese government in Hong Kong in 1997
    b. the change from Clinton's presidency to G.W. Bush's presidency
    c. the American Revolution

5. Where would you expect to see an <u>investigative reporter</u>?
    a. on a surprise visit to a 5-star restaurant to determine if it is meeting health codes
    b. covering a big football game such as the Super Bowl
    c. attending a local building dedication ceremony

Exercise 2

Some words have more than one meaning. Consider the various meanings of the words **correspond** and **correspondent**.

1. correspond (v) - to write to
2. correspond (v) - to agree, to match
3. correspondent (n) - a person to whom you write letters
4. correspondent (n) - a reporter for a publication or TV
5. correspondent (adj) - related to something

Use either 1, 2, 3, 4, or 5 to note which meaning is used in each sentence.

___ 1. Barbara Walters is a famous U.S. <u>correspondent</u> who works for a major television network.

___ 2. We have been <u>correspondents</u> ever since we were in the ninth grade.

___ 3. The amount of effort that you put into your work should bring a <u>correspondent</u> yearly pay raise.

___ 4. Her hair color <u>corresponds</u> to her eye color.

___ 5. We <u>correspond</u> regularly by electronic mail.

E. USING WORDS IN COMMUNICATION

Exercise 1

With a partner, discuss the following:

1. Describe your <u>transition</u> from high school to college studies.

2. Have you ever taken part in an <u>investigation</u>? When was it? What kind of <u>investigation</u> was it? If you haven't taken part in one, describe an <u>investigation</u> that you followed in the news or in your local community.

3. How would you <u>modify</u> a car or bicycle to meet your personal taste?

4. What is something that you do <u>constantly</u>? Why?

5. Name five countries and their <u>corresponding</u> capital cities.

Exercise 2

Role Play - Pretend that you are a journalist covering a big story, perhaps political in nature. Use all of the vocabulary words in this lesson (i.e. **constant, corresponding, investigation, modified,** and **transition**) to write a dialog between a journalist and his or her interviewee. Perform the dialog for your class.

REVIEW

Circle words and draw lines between words that you associate with each other. There is not one correct word association, and you may have more than one association with certain words and no associations with other words. Think about why you make these associations and be able to explain them to a partner.

project   alternative

                rejected

transition   medical

                sum

emerged   sustainable

                external

constant   styles

                image

investigation   fundamental

                option

modified   contribution

                dominant

license   corresponding

UNIT 4

WORDS

apparent	domestic	integration	proportion
aware	ethnic	logic	resolution
clause	evolution	network	sufficient
considerable	grant	objective	symbolic
decline	instance	overall	version

READINGS

Integration of Public Schools
Domestic Abuse
Evolution
Bending the Rules

STRATEGIES AND SKILLS

Word Forms
- Word family charts
- Word form selection

Comprehension Check
- Matching definitions
- Understanding and using words in context
- Identifying synonyms

Word Expansion
- Multiple meanings
- Collocations
- Grammar applications
- Suffixes

Interactive Speaking Practice
- Sentence completion
- Ranking priorities
- Listing
- Idiom usage
- Role play
- Associations

ACADEMIC WORD POWER

LESSON 1

A. WORD FAMILIES

Study the five word families below. Then fill in the word form chart. The underlined word forms at the top of the list are the most commonly used forms in academic texts.

integration	considerable	resolution	decline (2X)	aware
/ˌɪntəˈgreɪʃən/	/kənˈsɪdərəbəl/	/ˌrɛzəˈluʃən/	/dɪˈklaɪn/	/əˈwɛr/
integrate	considerably	resolve	declining	awareness
integrated		resolved		unaware
		unresolved		

Exercise - Word Form Chart

NOUN	VERB	ADJECTIVE	ADVERB
1. integration	1.	1.	
		1. considerable	1.
1. resolution	1.	1. 2.	
1. decline	1.	1.	
1.		1. aware 2.	

B. READING

Integration of Public Schools

In the 1950's, African-Americans struggled to secure civil rights for minorities in the U.S. Key to their goal of equality was <u>integration</u> of public schools. At that time, black students and white students attended different schools, which were supposedly separate but equal. However, activists fought to make policymakers <u>aware</u> that their schools were separate but not equal. There was a <u>considerable</u> difference in the amount of tax money spent on black students and white students. As a result, black schools were in poor repair and had too few resources to produce competitive graduates. A <u>resolution</u> of the conflict between blacks and whites was required in order to bring the students together to study in the same facilities. Nevertheless, a <u>decline</u> in black-white relations followed the initial attempts at <u>integration</u> of the schools. Many whites had little interest in furthering the cause of black equality. Consequently, it is taking years to achieve the goal of integration.

C. COMPREHENSION CHECK
Exercise 1
Refer to the previous reading and use the context to guess the meaning of the words below. Then match the words to their definitions. Do NOT use a dictionary.

___ 1. integration	A.	knowledgeable about
___ 2. considerable	B.	a final solution to a problem
___ 3. resolution	C.	putting different groups of people together
___ 4. decline	D.	deterioration, lowering, weakening
___ 5. aware	E.	much, a lot

Exercise 2
True or False? Write T or F in the blanks provided.

___ 1. Widespread use of the Internet could lead to a <u>decline</u> in newspaper subscriptions.

___ 2. A university education is a <u>considerable</u> investment in one's future.

___ 3. Airlines are <u>aware</u> of the public's frustration with airline service; therefore, airlines are attempting to improve.

___ 4. Diplomats sometimes use negotiations to find a peaceful <u>resolution</u> to the problems between two countries.

___ 5. If you are married to someone from a different race, you probably believe that <u>integration</u> of society is not a worthy goal.

D. WORD STUDY
Exercise
Choose the correct word form for each blank.

1. Many U.S. schools still haven't been properly _____. Often, Whites still go to predominantly white schools, and Blacks and Hispanics go to predominantly minority schools.
   a. integration   b. integrate   c. integrated

2. This university is _____ larger than it was ten years ago.
   a. considerable   b. consider   c. considerably

3. Their dispute is still _____. They cannot agree on who will receive which portion of the estate.
   a. resolution   b. resolved   c. unresolved

4. The building is in _____ condition; the windowpanes have been broken, and it is just a matter of time before the frame collapses.
   a. decline   b. declining

5. In order to effectively combat the threat of HIV, people must work to raise _____ about this menacing disease.
   a. aware   b. awareness   c. unaware

E. USING WORDS IN COMMUNICATION
Exercise 1
Repeat and complete the following sentences:

1. In my hometown, <u>integration</u> is evident at/in...

2. I have spent a <u>considerable</u> amount of time on...

3. My next New Year's <u>resolution</u> will be to...

4. There has been a <u>decline</u> in the sale of...

5. Most people are <u>unaware</u> of...

Exercise 2
Ranking - You and your partner are on the local school board. Your task is to prioritize the issues under consideration this year. Rank the following issues in order of importance. Which is the most important issue and which is the least?

____ 1. <u>integration</u> of minorities into mainly white schools

____ 2. <u>decline</u> in the facilities (i.e., the buildings need repairs)

____ 3. community <u>awareness</u> of the importance of primary education

____ 4. passing a <u>resolution</u> to keep children off of drugs

____ 5. the <u>considerable</u> expense of upgrading the school computers

Lesson 2

A. WORD FAMILIES

Study the five word families below. Then fill in the word form chart. The underlined word forms at the top of the list are the most commonly used forms in academic texts.

domestic (2X)	ethnic	network (2X)	version	proportion
/dəˈmɛstɪk/	/ˈɛθnɪk/	/ˈnɛtˌwɜrk/	/ˈvɜrʒən/	/prəˈpɔrʃən/
domestically	ethnicity			proportional
domesticate				proportionally
domesticated				proportionate
				proportionately
				disproportion
				disproportionate
				disproportionately

Exercise - Word Form Chart

NOUN	VERB	ADJECTIVE	ADVERB
1.	1.	1. domestic 2.	1.
1.		1. ethnic	
1.	1. network		
1. proportion 2.		1. 2. 3.	1. 2. 3.
1. version			

B. READING

Domestic Abuse

Domestic abuse is a serious problem in the United States. It is not limited to particular groups; families from all ethnic backgrounds and social classes experience violence in the home. A larger proportion of the victims of this abuse are women. Victims frequently network, offering a support system in order to assist each other after bouts of violence. Complaints are often heard by the police, but the abusers' and the victims' versions of the events surrounding the abuse are rarely the same. Thus, it is difficult for police to do much in cases of domestic abuse; as a result, victims often stay with their abusers and continue to be beaten and humiliated for years.

C. COMPREHENSION CHECK
Exercise 1
Refer to the previous reading and use the context to guess the meaning of the words below. Then match the words to their definitions. Do NOT use a dictionary.

___ 1. domestic

___ 2. ethnic

___ 3. network

___ 4. proportion

___ 5. versions

A. relation of parts to one another, percentage

B. related to group characteristics, such as race, country of origin, or culture

C. accounts of something; slightly-revised copies

D. related to one's home life or home country

E. to meet and exchange information with people

Exercise 2
If the italicized word is used correctly in the sentence, write YES in the blank. If it is not used correctly, write NO in the blank.

_____ 1. A small <u>proportion</u> of the people in the United States are Native Americans.

_____ 2. <u>Domestic</u> flights at an airport leave from the international terminal.

_____ 3. It is important to <u>network</u> when you are looking for a job.

_____ 4. New <u>versions</u> of Microsoft Windows become available when improvements are made.

_____ 5. <u>Ethnic</u> conflicts are common among some tribes in Indonesia.

D. WORD STUDY
Exercise 1
Most words have more than one meaning. Consider the various meanings of the word **network**.

> 1. network (n) - a system of connected travel routes or communication lines
>
> 2. network (n) - a large television or radio company with stations across the country
>
> 3. network (v) - to meet and exchange information with people in one's profession, especially in order to further one's career

Use either 1, 2, or 3 to indicate which meaning is used in each sentence.

___ 1. CNN is the most-watched <u>network</u> of ex-patriots from the United States.

___ 2. It is of utmost importance for young people to <u>network</u> when they first get started in their careers.

___ 3. The existing <u>network</u> of satellites must be upgraded.

___ 4. The FBI has been trying to tap into the terrorists' <u>network</u>.

Exercise 2

These are some common collocations for words in this unit.

domestic dispute	ethnic minority	supply network
sizeable proportion	movie version	

Circle the letter of the correct answers for these collocations.

1. Which of the following is an example of a <u>domestic dispute</u>?

   a. the American Civil War

   b. World War II

   c. the Persian Gulf War

2. Which of the following is *not* an <u>ethnic minority</u> in the United States?

   a. African-Americans

   b. European-Americans

   c. Jewish-Americans

3. What is the correct order of a <u>supply network</u>?

   a. retailer – manufacturer – wholesaler — consumer

   b. consumer – wholesaler – retailer – manufacturer

   c. manufacturer – wholesaler – retailer – consumer

4. Which of the following pets can be found in a <u>sizeable proportion</u> of U.S. households?

   a. dogs

   b. rats

   c. snakes

E. USING WORDS IN COMMUNICATION
Exercise 1

1. List 3 television <u>networks</u> in the United States.

2. List 3 books for which you can find a movie <u>version</u>.

3. List 3 <u>ethnicities</u> of people who live in the world.

4. List 3 airlines that fly <u>domestic</u> routes.

Exercise 2

Idioms - Consider this idiomatic usage of the word **proportion**.

Mary is a hard worker who takes her job seriously, but she has <u>a sense of proportion</u> and finds time to have fun.

John got very jealous when his wife, Julie, spoke to another man at a party. She grew weary of his jealous whining and urged him not <u>to blow</u> the incident <u>out of proportion</u>; all she had done was talk to the man, nothing more.

With your partner, discuss these idioms. Write what you think the idioms mean here.

"a sense of proportion" –

"to blow out of proportion" –

Check your answers with another pair of students. When you think you know what the idioms mean, discuss the following questions.

1. When was the last time you blew some small problem out of proportion?
   Describe the incident to your partner.

2. When it comes to studying, do you have a good sense of proportion?
   Do you study hard but still find time to socialize?

LESSON 3

A. WORD FAMILIES

Study the five word families below. Then fill in the word form chart. The underlined word forms at the top of the list are the most commonly used forms in academic texts.

evolution	grant (2X)	logic	overall	sufficient
/ˌɛvəˈluʃən/	/grænt/	/ˈlɑdʒɪk/	/ˌouvərˈɔl/	/səˈfɪʃənt/
evolve		logical		sufficiency
evolved		logically		insufficient
evolving		logician		insufficiently
evolutionary		illogical		sufficiently
evolutionist		illogically		

Exercise - Word Form Chart

NOUN	VERB	ADJECTIVE	ADVERB
1. evolution 2.	1.	1. 2. 3.	
1.	1. grant		
1. logic 2.		1. 2.	1. 2.
		1. overall	
1.		1. sufficient 2.	1. 2.

B. READING

Evolution

Despite much evidence in support of the theory of <u>evolution</u>, there are still many people who refuse to believe that human beings evolved from a lesser life form into the creatures they are today. Some people claim that there is not <u>sufficient</u> evidence to support the idea that humans are a form of ape. <u>Granted</u>, it is a difficult concept to grasp. It is not easy to see the <u>logic</u> of a progression from sea creatures to land-dwelling hunters and gatherers to men who walk upright. If we look around us, all these types of creatures are still in existence, so many people fail to see how humans could ever have been lesser life forms. However, the <u>overall</u> consensus among the scientific community is that evolution is an indisputable fact, not just a theory.

C. COMPREHENSION CHECK
Exercise 1
Refer to the previous reading and use the context to guess the meaning of the words below. Then match the words to their definitions. Do NOT use a dictionary.

___ 1. evolution		A.	the development of living things
___ 2. granted		B.	general, considering everything
___ 3. logic		C.	accepted as true; given
___ 4. overall		D.	ample, enough
___ 5. sufficient		E.	a system of reasoning

Exercise 2
Fill in the blanks using the appropriate vocabulary word.

1. His grade point average in his major was much higher than his _____ grade point average.
2. Charles Darwin is credited with the Theory of _____.
3. Dr. Spock urged his math students to use _____ when they were approaching new problems.
4. They do not have a _____ amount of time and resources to finish this project.
5. Santa Claus promised those children that their wishes would be _____.

D. WORD STUDY
Exercise 1
Choose the correct word form for each blank.

1. Apes are more highly _____ than monkeys. Their reasoning skills are better, and their social interactions are more complex.
   a. evolution   b. evolutionary   c. evolved

2. The graduate student was given a large _____ for his research project.
   a. granted   b. grant   c. granting

3. It was obvious to the other scientists that there was a flaw in Dr. Zu's _____; no one else could reach the conclusions that he did.
   a. logic   b. logical   c. logically

4. The doctor was not _____ convinced that his patient required a full frontal lobotomy. As a result, he merely prescribed shock therapy.
   a. sufficient   b. sufficiency   c. sufficiently

Exercise 2

Find the errors in the following sentences and correct them.

1. Chimpanzees are said to be more highly evolution than mice.

   (1 mistake)

2. When something are familiar and reliable, it is said to be "taken for grant."

   (2 mistakes)

3. There is a character on the TV show *Star Trek* who is famous for his use of logical.

   (1 mistake)

4. They could not buy the house because they had insufficiently funds.

   (1 mistake)

E. USING WORDS IN COMMUNICATION

Exercise 1

Answer the following:

1. Do you believe in the theory of <u>evolution</u>? Explain your answer.

2. If a genie could <u>grant</u> you one wish, what would you wish for?

3. Some people say that women are emotional while men are <u>logical</u>.
   Do you agree or disagree? Explain your answer.

4. What is your <u>overall</u> impression of this class?

5. How much income is <u>sufficient</u> for a decent standard of living?

Exercise 2

Role Play - Pretend that you and your partner are scientists. One of you has recently made a discovery about the origin of human beings. Discuss your findings using the vocabulary from this lesson; i.e., **evolution, granted, logical, overall, sufficient.**

LESSON 4

A. WORD FAMILIES

Study the five word families below. Then fill in the word form chart. The underlined word forms at the top of the list are the most commonly used forms in academic texts.

clause	apparent	instance	objective (2X)	symbolic
/klɔz/	/əˈpærənt/	/ˈɪnstəns/	/əbˈdʒɛktɪv/	/sɪmˈbɑlɪk/
	apparently		objectively	symbolically
			objectivity	symbolize
				symbolism
				symbol

Exercise - Word Form Chart

NOUN	VERB	ADJECTIVE	ADVERB
1. clause			
		1. apparent	1.
1. instance			
1. objective 2.		1.	1.
1. 2.	1.	1. symbolic	1.

B. READING

Bending the Rules

When Jack Smith signed the lease on his apartment, he foolishly neglected to read the document in its entirety. As a result, he was stunned when the apartment manager presented him with a bill for $75.00 for trash pick-up from his front porch. He had not read the <u>clause</u> in the lease stipulating that each tenant was responsible for taking his own trash to the dumpsters provided by the complex. Furthermore, failure to take trash out oneself, necessitating the services of an apartment complex employee, would result in a fine of $75.00. When Smith approached the apartment manager, his <u>objective</u> was to have the fine waived on the condition that he agree never to leave his trash on the front porch again. The manager agreed that for this <u>instance</u> and only this instance, he would waive the $75.00 fine. Jack's happiness about this decision was <u>apparent</u> as he shook the manager's hand and thanked him repeatedly. It was more than a <u>symbolic</u> victory; he had managed to save himself seventy-five hard-earned dollars.

C. COMPREHENSION CHECK
Exercise 1
Refer to the previous reading and use the context to guess the meaning of the words below. Then match the words to their definitions. Do NOT use a dictionary.

____	1. apparent	A.	a single occurrence or happening
____	2. clause	B.	not real, only for show
____	3. instance	C.	a part in a document that requires something to be done
____	4. objective	D.	a goal, purpose
____	5. symbolic	E.	obvious, clear

Exercise 2
Which word does not belong?

1.	apparently	sufficiently	seemingly	evidently
2.	clause	article	section	machine
3.	instance	celebration	occasion	moment
4.	objective	aim	intention	condition
5.	symbolic	concrete	figurative	representative

D. WORD STUDY
Exercise
Most words have more than one meaning. Consider the meanings of the word **objective**.

---

1. objective (adj.) – not influenced by emotions or personal beliefs, fair

2. objective (adj.) – existing outside the mind, real

3. objective (n) – a goal, purpose

Use either 1, 2, or 3 to note which meaning is used in each sentence.

____ 1. It is difficult to be <u>objective</u> when judging the work of one's friends or family.

____ 2. Al Gore had several <u>objectives</u> in mind when he ran for office. He wanted to champion the environment, improve the existing health care system, and extend prosperity to those who had not prospered through the nineties.

____ 3. In the 1960's, some people who experimented with psychedelic drugs argued that there was no <u>objective</u> reality; all experiences depended on one's individual perceptions.

____ 4. Foreign students sometimes argue that U.S. professors' grading policies are not <u>objective</u>. They want to see more standardization of tests and grades.

E. USING WORDS IN COMMUNICATION
Exercise 1

1. List 3 <u>apparent</u> improvements that need to be made in this classroom.

2. List 3 <u>objectives</u> you'd like to accomplish in your life.

3. List 3 things that <u>symbolize</u> winter.

4. List 3 <u>instances</u> in which you believe teachers should bend the rules for students.

Exercise 2 - Word Associations

In the chart below, write one word you associate with each of the words from this lesson. Then go around the classroom and see if anyone has one or more of the same words associated with the vocabulary words. If you find someone who does, sit with that classmate and discuss your associations. If you do not find a student with any of the same associations, choose a partner with whom to discuss your associations.

apparent	
clause	
instance	
objective	
symbolic	

REVIEW

Choose one word from the box to mplete each sentence.
Do not use the same word twice.

apparent	decline	grant	network	resolution
aware	domestic	instance	objective	sufficient
clause	ethnic	integration	overall	symbolic
considerable	evolution	logic	proportion	version

1. A group of connected computers is called a _____.
2. When something is falling apart, it is said to be in _____.
3. A short period of time in which something occurs is an _____.
4. A servant who works in a home can be called a _____.
5. After a conflict, there is usually a _____.
6. If groups of people are fighting about something related to their religion or back ground, their conflict is called _____.
7. When you have enough of something, you say that is _____.
8. When something represents something else, it is said to be _____ of that thing.
9. A goal or an aim is also called an _____.
10. The genie said that Aladdin's wishes would be _____.
11. Mathematics requires use of _____.
12. The act of bringing people or things together is called _____.
13. If a man has four billion dollars and another man has only four thousand, then the difference between their bank accounts is _____.
14. If something is obvious, it is _____.
15. If you know about something, then you are _____ of it.
16. He wrote the paper in one style for his English professor, but he wrote a different _____ of   the paper for his comparative literature professor.
17. If a bill includes everything purchased, then it is an _____ account of what you bought.
18. The amount of money you earn should be in direct _____ to the amount of work you do.
19. The idea that humans evolved from a lower life form is called the theory of _____.
20. One part, with its own subject and verb, of a complex or compound sentence is a _____.

UNIT 5

WORDS

adjustment	convention	hypothesis	notion
author	display	intelligence	orientation
brief	equivalent	lecture	pursue
civil	fee	liberal	statistic
commitment	flexibility	minimum	stability

READINGS

Freshman Year
A Spy's Job
Professor Trippet's Wacky Hypothesis
An Enviable Profession

STRATEGIES AND SKILLS

Word Forms
- Word family charts
- Word form selection

Comprehension Check
- Matching definitions
- Understanding words in context
- Identifying synonyms

Word Expansion
- Suffixes
- Multiple meanings
- Collocations

Interactive Speaking Practice
- Sentence completion
- Listing
- Associations
- Story writing

ACADEMIC WORD POWER

LESSON 1

A. WORD FAMILIES

Study the five word families below. Then fill in the word form chart. The underlined word forms at the top of the list are the most commonly used forms in academic texts.

<u>fee</u>	<u>orientation</u>	<u>liberal</u> (2X)	<u>adjustment</u>	<u>stability</u>
/fi/	/ˌɔriən'teɪʃən/	/'lɪbərəl/	/ə'dʒʌstmənt/	/stə'bɪləti/
	orient	liberalize	adjust	stable
	reorient	liberate	readjust	instability
		liberated	readjustment	stabilize
		liberation		stabilization
		liberator		unstable
		liberally		

Exercise - Word Form Chart

NOUN	VERB	ADJECTIVE	ADVERB
1. fee			
1. orientation	1. 2.		
1. 2. 3.	1. 2.	1. liberal 2.	1.
1. adjustment 2.	1. 2.		
1. stability 2. 3.	1.	1. 2.	

B. READING

Freshman Year

In the freshman year at the university, students go through a period of <u>adjustment</u>. For many students, it is their first experience of living away from home. Thus, most universities offer an <u>orientation</u> at the beginning of the semester during which students are taught about the university's facilities, course offerings, regulations, how to pay tuition and <u>fees</u>, and other information essential to the university student. Many students who have not yet chosen a major course of study learn about the differences between liberal arts, business, and the natural sciences. It takes quite some time before the newness and confusion of university life wears off and a sense of <u>stability</u> sets in. After new students grow accustomed to a <u>liberal</u> amount of free time, and they become used to their new environment, most of them enjoy university life.

C. COMPREHENSION CHECK
Exercise 1
Refer to the previous reading and use the context to guess the meaning of the words below. Then match the words to their definitions. Do NOT use a dictionary.

___ 1. fees   A. a state of very little change or upset
___ 2. orientation   B. a period of becoming familiar with a new situation
___ 3. liberal   C. a change, an adaptation
___ 4. adjustment   D. generous, large
___ 5. stability   E. charge, cost

Exercise 2
True or False? Write T or F in the blanks provided.

___ 1. The 1990's was a period of relative <u>stability</u> for the USA due to the economic boom during those years.
___ 2. <u>Orientations</u> for new employees can be very useful.
___ 3. <u>Fees</u> for parking permits are optional fees, but course <u>fees</u> for students are mandatory.
___ 4. <u>Liberal</u> helpings of turkey are served at Thanksgiving dinners.
___ 5. <u>Adjustment</u> to a new baby in a household is always easy.

D. WORD STUDY
Exercise 1
Choose the correct word form for each blank.

1. When workers have been working for a long time at a particular job and a major change takes place in the company, the old workers have to undergo a _____ so that they can learn all about the new changes.
   a. orient   b. reorientation   c. reorient

2. Whenever a war ends, soldiers must enter prisons and _____ the prisoners.
   a. liberalize   b. liberate   c. liberally

3. If a father leaves his family for a long period of time and then comes back, he has to _____ to the household dynamic.
   a. adjustment   b. adjusted   c. readjust

4. After the building burned down, survivors of the fire suffered from an acute sense of _____.
   a. stability   b. instability   c. unstable

5. Renee and Bob did not realize there would be so many _____ involved in buying a house. When they learned how expensive it would buy a house, they decided to ask their parents for help.
   a. fee   b. fees

Exercise 2

Most words have more than one meaning. Consider the various meanings of the word **liberal**.

> 1. liberal (n) - a person or politician of progressive views
>
> 2. liberal (adj) - generous, large
>
> 3. liberal (adj) - proposing change, progressive

Use either 1, 2, or 3 to note which meaning is used in each sentence.

___ 1. A philanthropist is usually <u>liberal</u> with his checkbook.

___ 2. Republicans were always accusing Bill Clinton of being a <u>liberal</u> when, in fact, he was quite a centrist.

___ 3. My grandmother is unusually <u>liberal</u> in her way of thinking; it is not so common for old people to welcome change.

___ 4. When asked if he was a <u>liberal</u> or a conservative, he replied that he was neither; rather, he called himself an independent.

___ 5. She stored a <u>liberal</u> supply of cookies in the pantry in case children dropped by for a visit.

E. USING WORDS IN COMMUNICATION
Exercise 1

Repeat and complete the following sentences:

1. Course <u>fees</u> are …

2. We could use an <u>orientation</u> session on …

3. Some <u>liberal</u> ideas I agree/disagree with are …

4. I went through a period of <u>adjustment</u> when …

5. A time of <u>stability</u> in my life was...

Exercise 2 - Lists

1. List 3 <u>unstable</u> people you have known.

2. List 3 <u>liberal</u> politicians.

3. List 3 <u>adjustments</u> that should be made to your English class.

4. List 3 <u>fees</u> you pay that you believe are unreasonably high.

LESSON 2

A. WORD FAMILIES

Study the five word families below. Then fill in the word form chart. The underlined word forms at the top of the list are the most commonly used forms in academic texts.

brief (3X)	civil	pursue	intelligence	minimum (2X)
/brif/	/'sɪvəl/	/pər'su/	/ɪn'tɛlədʒəns/	/'mɪnəməm/
brevity	civilian	pursuit	intelligent	minimal
briefly			intelligently	
			unintelligent	

Exercise - Word Form Chart

NOUN	VERB	ADJECTIVE	ADVERB
1. 2.	1.	1. brief	1.
1.		1. civil	
1.	1. pursue		
1. intelligence		1. 2.	1.
1. minimum		1. 2.	

B. READING

A Spy's Job

Military <u>intelligence</u> is a division of the armed services that spies on enemies or potential enemies. This division usually knows when a <u>civil</u> war is going to take place in a country because a spy's job is to find out important information —both internal and external— concerning foreign governments. Once they learn secret information, spies have to give their superior officers a <u>brief</u> summary of the potential danger that a situation might pose to other countries. However, because of the high level of secrecy surrounding such important matters of state, spies usually learn a bare <u>minimum</u> of information concerning a potential <u>civil</u> war or attack on a foreign enemy. Because of the complexity of the job, it requires a high degree of <u>intelligence</u>. Spies must be smart as they constantly <u>pursue</u> new information about the country and the leaders of the country to which they are assigned. A spy's work is difficult.

C. COMPREHENSION CHECK
Exercise 1
Refer to the previous reading above and use the context to guess the meaning of the words below. Then match the words to their definitions. Do NOT use a dictionary.

____ 1. intelligence
____ 2. civil
____ 3. brief
____ 4. pursue
____ 5. minimum

A. of citizens in general, not religious or military
B. short, to the point
C. to go after
D. the least amount of something
E. 1) secret information about a country or an enemy;
   2) ability to learn and understand information

Exercise 2
If the italicized word is used correctly in the sentence, write YES in the blank. If it is not used correctly, write NO in the blank.

____ 1. Martin Luther King, Jr. was a famous civil rights leader.
____ 2. The President gave a brief speech at the memorial service.
____ 3. The actress pursued the role until the director gave in and gave it to her.
____ 4. Dan did not have much money for Christmas shopping. The minimum he could spend on each gift was $1000.
____ 5. Trees have a high degree of intelligence.

D. WORD STUDY
Exercise 1
These are some common collocations for the adjective **civil**.

1. civil war - a war between groups in a country
2. civil rights - in the United States, the rights of each citizen such as the rights to vote and not be discriminated against, guaranteed by the U.S. Constitution
3. civil law - the body of law dealing with the rights of individual citizens
4. civil service - government employees and the governmental work that they do

Fill in the blank using the correct word from the list above.

1. Citizens' civil _____ are guaranteed in the U.S. Constitution.
2. Sierra Leone has suffered from years of civil _____.
3. The Civil _____ was the bloodiest conflict in U.S. history.
4. In many countries, a civil _____ job is considered a good career.
5. Detaining citizens without charging them for a specific crime is a violation of civil _____.
6. Rosa Parks' refusal to yield her seat sparked the beginning of the Civil _____ Movement in the United States.

Exercise 2
These are some common collocations for words in this unit.

brief silence	bare minimum	civil disobedience	constant pursuit

Circle the letter of the correct answers for these collocations.

1. When someone is arrested for <u>civil disobedience</u>, what might he or she have been arrested for?

   a. killing someone

   b. publicly protesting a law which they feel is unfair

   c. attacking someone and stealing his money

2. In which situation might a <u>brief silence</u> be appropriate?

   a. a funeral

   b. a birthday party

   c. a music concert

3. Which student did the <u>bare minimum</u> to pass his history course?

   a. the student who attended every lecture and visited his professor during office hours every week

   b. the student who skipped the lectures and only took the exams, passing them with a C- average

   c. the student who studied every day and memorized all new concepts

4. If a detective is in <u>constant pursuit</u> of a criminal, how often does he let the case rest?

   a. once a month

   b. once a week

   c. never

E. USING WORDS IN COMMUNICATION
Exercise
Make 5 lists with the new vocabulary words and the words you associate with them. Then cut up your lists, and see if your partner can put the lists back together again. The words are:
brief, civil, intelligence, pursue, and **minimum.**

LESSON 3

A. WORD FAMILIES

Study the five word families below. Then fill in the word form chart. The underlined word forms at the top of the list are the most commonly used forms in academic texts.

hypothesis	lecture (2X)	notion	statistic	equivalent (2X)
/haɪˈpɑθəsɪs/	/ˈlɛktʃər/	/ˈnouʃən/	/stəˈtɪstɪk/	/ɪˈkwɪvələnt/
hypothesize	lecturer		statistician	equivalence
hypothetical			statistical	
hypothetically			statistically	

Exercise - Word Form Chart

NOUN	VERB	ADJECTIVE	ADVERB
1. hypothesis	1.	1.	1.
1. lecture 2.	1.		
1. notion			
1. statistic 2.		1.	1.
1. equivalent 2.		1.	

B. READING

Professor Trippet's Wacky Hypothesis

Professor Trippet is a very popular lecturer at the University of Southfield. He is famous for his theory of *Habilium sepicum*, about which many articles have been published in various magazines and journals. The theory has to do with the notion that people are essentially the equivalent of ants living in a universe much larger than the one that human beings can perceive with their limited senses. Professor Trippet receives lots of criticism from the scientific community because his hypothesis cannot be tested in a laboratory, and there are not any statistics available to support his theories. However, students are fascinated by his outlandish ideas, as evidenced by the high level of attendance at each of his lectures.

C. COMPREHENSION CHECK

Exercise 1

Refer to the reading above and use the context to guess the meaning of the words below. Then match the words to their definitions. Do NOT use a dictionary.

___ 1. lectures		A.	collection of numerical information
___ 2. hypothesis		B.	speeches on a topic
___ 3. notion		C.	a belief, idea or opinion
___ 4. statistics		D.	something that is the same, equal
___ 5. equivalent		E.	an idea that explains something but has not yet been proven

Exercise 2

Which word does not belong?

1.	lecture	article	address	talk
2.	hypothesis	theory	guess	fact
3.	notion	concept	occasion	thought
4.	statistics	data	numbers	utensils
5.	equivalent	dissimilar	corresponding	alike

D. WORD STUDY

Exercise

These are some common collocations for words in this unit.

> reasonable hypothesis – an idea put forth by a scientist or researcher that appeals to common sense
>
> vague notion - having less than a basic understanding about something of which you have little experience.
> *For example, the average high school graduate might have a vague notion about Einstein's Theory of Relativity. That is, he may be able to identify it as e=mc², but he does not really know what it means.*
>
> moral equivalent – something equal to another in a moral sense.
> *For example, some persons consider capital punishment to be the moral equivalent of murder.*

Answer these questions:

1. In your opinion, is there a <u>moral equivalent</u> to Mahatma Gandhi's non-violence practices? Explain.
2. Is there some branch of science about which you have not the <u>vaguest notion</u>? Which branch of science (i.e., astrophysics, metaphysics, zoology) is it?
3. What is a <u>reasonable hypothesis</u> for how the Earth was formed?

E. USING WORDS IN COMMUNICATION

Exercise 1

Answer the following:

1. Do you believe that <u>statistics</u> can lie? Explain your answer.

2. Discuss your own <u>hypothesis</u> about where humans first appeared on planet Earth. Was it Asia, Africa, Europe, or many places at once? Explain.

3. Is there a <u>notion</u> (i.e., the idea that there is life on other planets) that you find completely ridiculous? If so, what is it?

4. How do you feel about <u>lecturing</u> as a teaching method? Do you find that attending <u>lectures</u> is a good way to learn new information?

5. In the United States, American football is the most popular sport. What sport has the <u>equivalent</u> popularity in other countries?

Exercise 2

Using the five new vocabulary words (i.e., **statistics, equivalent, lecture, hypothesis, notion**), with a partner, write a paragraph or a story. Share your composition with the class.

LESSON 4

A. WORD FAMILIES

Study the five word families below. Then fill in the word form chart. The underlined word forms at the top of the list are the most commonly used forms in academic texts.

author (2X)	commitment	convention	flexibility	display (2X)
/'ɔθər/	/kə'mɪtmənt/	/kən'vɛnʃən/	/ˌflɛksə'bɪləti/	/dɪs'pleɪ/
authorship	commit	convene	flexible	
	committed	conventional	inflexible	
		conventionally	inflexibility	
		unconventional		

Exercise - Word Form Chart

NOUN	VERB	ADJECTIVE	ADVERB
1. author 2.	1.		
1. commitment	1.	1.	
1. convention	1.	1. 2.	1.
1. flexibility 2.		1. 2.	
1. display	1.		

B. READING

An Enviable Profession

Authors have an enviable profession. They write books and articles for publication, and they generally work at home. Published authors usually have a commitment to write several books for their publishers. However, there is much flexibility concerning what they can write about and when they have to submit their work. For example, an author might have a commitment to write and publish three books over a five-year period. What he writes about and when he writes the books is entirely up to him. Another perk of the profession is that authors get to travel a lot. For example, they attend writers' conventions where they meet other authors, and they go on book-signing tours, promoting their work at bookstores where their own books are on display. Nothing beats the writer's life.

C. COMPREHENSION CHECK
Exercise 1

Refer to the previous reading and use the context to guess the meaning of the words below. Then match the words to their definitions. Do NOT use a dictionary.

____ 1. authors		A.	the ability to bend easily or to be accommodating
____ 2. commitment		B.	people who write books, articles, or poems
____ 3. conventions		C.	gatherings where people of similar interests listen to speakers
____ 4. display		D.	something placed in a position to be seen
____ 5. flexibility		E.	a promise, an obligation

Exercise 2

True or False? Write T or F in the blanks provided.

____ 1. Michael Jordan is a famous <u>author</u>.

____ 2. People often learn new things at a <u>convention</u>.

____ 3. <u>Flexibility</u> is a desirable characteristic in an employee.

____ 4. Marriage is a <u>commitment</u> which should not be taken seriously.

____ 5. Companies <u>display</u> their products in grocery stores and shopping malls.

D. WORD STUDY
Exercise

Some words have more than one meaning. Consider the meanings of the word **convention**.

1. convention (n) – a gathering where people of similar interests listen to speakers
2. convention (n) – rule of behavior, a standard custom
3. convention (n) – a formal agreement among countries

Use either 1, 2, or 3 to note which meaning is used in each sentence.

____ 1. In the 1960s, hippies questioned and protested the <u>conventions</u> of U.S. society.

____ 2. The Geneva <u>Convention</u> is often mentioned in the news, especially in wartime.

____ 3. Every year around November 22, conspiracy theorists attend a <u>convention</u> on ideas about the assassination of John F. Kennedy.

E. USING WORDS IN COMMUNICATION

Exercise 1

Repeat and complete the following sentences:

1. My favorite <u>author</u> is…

2. The <u>commitment</u> I take most seriously in life is…

3. I would like to attend a <u>convention</u> on…

4. I always get hungry when I see a <u>display</u> of…

5. I cannot be <u>flexible</u> about…

Exercise 2

1. List 3 famous <u>authors</u>.

2. List 3 <u>conventions</u> that almost everybody observes.

3. List 3 <u>displays</u> of public affection.

4. List 3 people you have known who are <u>inflexible</u>.

5. List 3 <u>commitments</u> you have made in your life so far.

REVIEW

Match the sentence halves.

___ 1. The students attended a special <u>lecture</u>

___ 2. At a <u>convention</u> of mathematicians,

___ 3. In a <u>brief</u> statement,

___ 4. Sweatshirts which <u>displayed</u> the university's name

___ 5. A <u>civil</u> servant usually does not have much

___ 6. Because the student was overcharged for <u>fees,</u>

___ 7. Despite her high level of <u>intelligence,</u>

___ 8. Jim's <u>hypothesis</u> was accepted,

___ 9. <u>Stability</u> in marriage

___ 10. Her <u>liberal</u> use of colorful language

A. requires a strong <u>commitment</u> to the relationship.

B. <u>flexibility</u> in his work schedule.

C. were given away at freshman student <u>orientation</u>.

D. the accounting office had to make an <u>adjustment</u> to his financial aid records.

E. a speaker uses a <u>minimum</u> number of words.

F. which was given by a famous <u>author</u>.

G. made her report the <u>equivalent</u> of poetry or epic prose.

H. she had not the slightest <u>notion</u> of how to perform brain surgery.

I. <u>statistics</u> would be a popular topic for discussion.

J. so he was given permission to <u>pursue</u> his research further.

UNIT 6

ACADEMIC WORD POWER

LESSON 1

A. WORD FAMILIES

Study the five word families below. Then fill in the word form chart. The underlined word forms at the top of the list are the most commonly used forms in academic texts.

consultation	monitor (2X)	precise	prime (2X)	status
/ˌkɑnsəlˈteɪʃən/	/ˈmɑnətər/	/prɪˈsaɪs/	/praɪm/	/ˈstætəs/
consult	monitored	imprecise	primacy	/ˈsteɪtəs/
consultant	unmonitored	precisely		
consulting	monitoring	precision		

Exercise - Word Form Chart

Noun	Verb	Adjective	Adverb
1. consultation 2.	1.	1.	
1.	1. monitor	1. 2. 3.	
1.		1. precise 2.	1.
1.	1.	1. prime	
1. status			

B. READING

Prenatal Care

In the United States, women who become pregnant go through a nine-month period of prenatal care. From the time a woman suspects that she is pregnant, she begins a <u>consultation</u> with a physician or nurse midwife. Over the next several months, various devices for <u>monitoring</u> the <u>status</u> of the developing fetus are used. Tests can be done so that expectant mothers know the <u>precise</u> week when they got pregnant and when their child is due to be born. Although the <u>prime</u> years for pregnancy are in the early twenties to mid-thirties, because of the advanced level of prenatal care now available, women are able to bear children well into their forties with relatively few complications.

C. COMPREHENSION CHECK
Exercise 1

Refer to the reading above and use the context to guess the meaning of the words below. Then match the words to their definitions. Do NOT use a dictionary.

_____ 1. monitoring   A. exact, accurate

_____ 2. precise   B. the act of advising someone for pay

_____ 3. prime   C. checking on the performance of something

_____ 4. status   D. the situation of something at a particular time

_____ 5. consultation   E. the period in which a person is at the height of his or her abilities

Exercise 2

True or False? Write T or F in the blanks provided.

_____ 1. Michael Jordan is no longer in his <u>prime</u> basketball-playing years.

_____ 2. Weather forecasters always give the <u>precise</u> weather forecast.

_____ 3. Most lawyers are well paid for their <u>consultations</u> with clients.

_____ 4. Nurses are responsible for <u>monitoring</u> patients' vital signs.

_____ 5. The <u>status</u> of financial markets largely depends on the weather.

D. WORD STUDY
Exercise 1

Look at the chart below and try to guess the other meanings of the word **prime**.

1	2
Her <u>prime</u> concern now is raising her children. The carpenter <u>primed</u> the wood before he painted it a new color.	We had a wonderful dinner last night of <u>prime</u> beef ribs. We <u>primed</u> our daughter before her first day of school.

1. What does <u>prime</u> mean in the sentences in columns 1 and 2? How are these meanings similar?

2. What does <u>primed</u> mean in the sentences in columns 1 and 2? How are these meanings similar?

Exercise 2
Choose the correct word form for each blank.

1. Andrew is a well-paid _____ for high-tech companies who need freelance software engineers.
   a. consult   b. consultant   c. consultative

2. Some criminals on parole have _____ devices attached to their ankles so that their parole officers can know exactly where they are.
   a. monitor   b. monitoring

3. Computers can solve complex mathematical problems with a high level of _____.
   a. precise   b. precision   c. precisely

4. The cafeteria never serves _____ rib; the small food budget only allows for lesser cuts of meat.
   a. prime   b. primacy

E. USING WORDS IN COMMUNICATION
Exercise 1
Repeat and complete the following sentences:

1. I often check the status of...

2. Children should be closely monitored until the age of...

3. Some day I will purchase a prime...

4. The precise date and hour of my birth was...

5. I would consult a fortuneteller if...

Exercise 2
On a sheet of paper, write down several words that you associate with each of the vocabulary words in this lesson. When you finish, cut up your lists and give the words to your partner. She/He will give you hers/his. You and your partner must try to place the associated words under the right words from this lesson. Compare and discuss.

consult	monitor	precise	prime	status

LESSON 2

A. WORD FAMILIES

Study the five word families below. Then fill in the word form chart. The underlined word forms at the top of the list are the most commonly used forms in academic texts.

welfare	ignore	trend	justification	expert (2X)
/ˈwɛlˌfɛr/	/ɪgˈnɔr/	/trɛnd/	/ˌdʒʌstəfəˈkeɪʃən/	/ˈɛkˌspɜrt/
	ignorance		justify	expertise
	ignorant		justifiably	expertly
			justifiable	
			justified	
			unjustified	

Exercise - Word Form Chart

NOUN	VERB	ADJECTIVE	ADVERB
1. welfare			
1.	1. ignore	1.	
1. trend			
1. justification	1.	1. 2. 3.	1.
1. expert 2.		1.	1.

B. READING

Welfare

The poorest people in the United States are able to receive monthly checks from the government despite the fact that they do not work. This social benefit is called underline welfare because it is concerned with the well-being of the poor. For years, welfare recipients were ignored by most but targeted by a small minority who greatly resented seeing tax dollars spent on the upkeep of the poor. In the 1990s, a decade of great prosperity in the United States, it became a trend among conservative politicians to attack welfare recipients as lazy and overly dependent on others for their living. Even many left-leaning politicians who had previously offered justifications for welfare were now no longer convinced of the need for this controversial program. As a result, experts were asked to think of a way to get people off of welfare and into the workplace. During former U.S. President Bill Clinton's first administration, major welfare reform was initiated. Today welfare still exists, but it has been greatly reduced so that fewer people take advantage of the benefit, and they cannot receive it for an unlimited time.

C. COMPREHENSION CHECK
Exercise 1
Refer to the previous reading and use the context to guess the meaning of the words below. Then match the words to their definitions. Do NOT use a dictionary.

____ 1. welfare

____ 2. trend

____ 3. ignored

____ 4. experts

____ 5. justifications

A. a fashion, current style

B. 1) money from the government for food, housing, health services, etc.; 2) one's general condition

C. not paid attention to, overlooked

D. good reasons for doing something

E. masters at something, authority

Exercise 2
Match the clauses on the left with those that complete them on the right.

____ 1. If you receive <u>welfare</u> checks,

____ 2. If you are <u>ignored</u> by your parents,

____ 3. If you can offer a <u>justification</u> for something,

____ 4. If <u>experts</u> agree with you,

____ 5. If you follow <u>trends</u> closely,

A. you are very aware of the current fashions.

B. you have an acceptable excuse.

C. you must be very knowledgeable about a topic.

D. you are probably very lonely.

E. you must not have a well-paid job.

D. WORD STUDY
Exercise 1
Reread the reading at the beginning of this lesson. Make a list of all the words that go with welfare. Add others if you can think of any.

1. _____ *welfare check* _____

2. _____

3. _____

4. _____

5. _____

Exercise 2
Choose the correct word form for each blank.

1. Many people cannot help being _____ ; there are no schools available in their areas, so there is no place to learn.
   a. ignored   b. ignorant   c. ignorance

2. In the United States, sometimes a crime of passion is considered _____, and the criminal is not punished.
   a. justify   b. justifiable   c. justifiably

3. Because Phillip was chronically depressed, his family urged him to seek _____ advice.
   a. expert   b. expertise   c. expertly.

E. USING WORDS IN COMMUNICATION

Exercise 1
In the chart below, write one word you associate with each of the words from this lesson. Then go around the classroom and see if anyone has one or more of the same words associated with the vocabulary words. If you find someone who does, sit with that classmate and discuss your associations. If you do not find a student with any of the same associations, choose a partner with whom to discuss your associations.

welfare	
trend	
ignored	
expert	
justification	

Exercise 2 - Lists

1. List 3 forms of <u>welfare</u> that people can receive.
2. List 3 fashion <u>trends</u> that have occurred in the last 12 months.
3. List 3 topics on which you would like to be an <u>expert</u>.
   For example, I would like to be an <u>expert</u> on English grammar.
4. List 3 <u>justifications</u> for immigrating to a foreign country.
5. List 3 people or types of people whom you have <u>ignored</u> in the past.

LESSON 3

A. WORD FAMILIES

Study the five word families below. Then fill in the word form chart. The underlined word forms at the top of the list are the most commonly used forms in academic texts.

capacity	dimension	perspective	instruction	draft (3X)
/kəˈpæsəti/	/dəˈmɛnʃən/	/pərˈspɛktɪv/	/ɪnˈstrʌkʃən/	/dræft/
incapacitate	dimensional		instruct	redraft
incapacitated	multidimensional		instructive	
			instructor	

Exercise - Word Form Chart

NOUN	VERB	ADJECTIVE	ADVERB
1. capacity	1.	1.	
1. dimension		1. 2.	
1. perspective			
1. instruction 2.	1.	1.	
1.	1. draft 2.	1.	

B. READING

Architects

Buildings are usually designed by architects. These professionals have an informed <u>perspective</u> on how a building should look so that it fits well into the surrounding area. When given an assignment to design a new building, an architect must consider the <u>instructions</u> of the client and the purpose of a particular building. He has to assess the <u>dimensions</u> of the building based on the space allotted for its existence. He must also consider the <u>capacity</u> of the building. That is, how many offices or rooms will the building contain, and how exactly are these rooms going to be placed? With these and other variables to consider, an architect must <u>draft</u> a blueprint for the building and present it to the client. Multiple drafts must be drawn before a design is finally agreed upon, at which point the project goes to a builder, who is responsible for actually constructing the architect's design.

C. COMPREHENSION CHECK

Exercise 1

Refer to the reading above and use the context to guess the meaning of the words below. Then match the words to their definitions. Do NOT use a dictionary.

_____ 1. draft   A. to draw the plans for something

_____ 2. perspective   B. measurements

_____ 3. instructions   C. a way of seeing things

_____ 4. dimensions   D. the greatest amount that something can contain

_____ 5. capacity   E. information about how to do something

Exercise 2

Which word does not belong?

1.	draft	outline	integrate	sketch
2.	perspective	area	viewpoint	angle
3.	instructions	directions	orders	destructions
4.	dimensions	science	proportion	size
5.	capacity	volume	space	movement

D. WORD STUDY

Exercise

Study the multiple meanings of the vocabulary words, and then do the exercise that follows.

> 1. draft (n) - one version of something written
> 2. draft (n) - a system of requiring people by law to serve in the military
> 3. draft (n) - air currents that chill the body
> 4. draft (v) - to write a version of something
> 5. draft (v) - to draw the plans for something
> 6. draft (v) - to require military service of someone
> 7. draft (adj) - used for pulling heavy loads

> 8. perspective (n) - in art, a manner of drawing objects to create a realistic sense of depth and distance in a space
> 9. perspective (n) - a way of seeing things, point of view
> 10. perspective (n) - the set of beliefs, interests, and attitudes that contribute to one's judgment on issues and events
> 11. perspective (n) - a position on a mountain or hill from which one can see a long way off

Write YES if the underlined word is used correctly or NO if it is used incorrectly.

_____ 1. My father was <u>drafted</u> during the Second World War.

_____ 2. Sara's <u>perspective</u> gave her a rare form of breast cancer.

_____ 3. Those donkeys have always been used as <u>draft</u> animals.

_____ 4. Chinese artists use <u>perspective</u> very differently from Western artists.

_____ 5. His loss of <u>perspective</u> led him to join the cult.

_____ 6. Her cheeks need a <u>draft</u> of color.

E. USING WORDS IN COMMUNICATION
Exercise 1
Answer the following.

1. What would you do if you were <u>drafted</u> into military service?

2. What are the <u>dimensions</u> of the ideal house? How many square meters should it have? How high should the ceilings be?

3. What is the <u>capacity</u> of your stomach? How many eggs can you eat in one meal? How much meat can you consume at one time?

4. Do you always read the <u>instructions</u> when you buy something new? Why or why not?

5. What is your <u>perspective</u> on the current economic situation in the U.S.A.?

Exercise 2
Role Play - Pretend that you are hiring an architect to build your dream home. You are the client and your partner is the architect. Give him <u>directions</u> about what to build. Tell him your <u>perspective</u> on how the house should be designed. Describe the <u>dimensions</u> that you envision for the house. Give him a deadline for a first <u>draft</u> of the blueprint. The architect should ask lots of questions using the vocabulary words as often as possible.

LESSON 4

A. WORD FAMILIES

Study the five word families below. Then fill in the word form chart. The underlined word forms at the top of the list are the most commonly used forms in academic texts.

adequate	attach	revenue	substitution	furthermore
/ˈædəkwɪt/	/əˈtætʃ/	/ˈrɛvəˌnu/	/ˌsʌbstɪˈtuʃən/	/ˈfɜrðərˌmɔr/
adequacy	attachment		substitute (3X)	
adequately				
inadequately				
inadequacy				
inadequate				

Exercise - Word Form Chart

NOUN	VERB	ADJECTIVE	ADVERB
1. 2.		1. adequate 2.	1. 2.
1.	1. attach		
1. revenue			
1. substitution 2.	1.	1.	
			1. furthermore

B. READING

Luigi's Restaurant

When Luigi Corleone opened a small Italian restaurant, he had no previous experience of running a small business. However, when his uncle heard that Luigi had an idea to open an old-style Italian restaurant, he offered him a lovely space <u>attached</u> to a popular clothing store which many Italian-Americans frequented. The space was inexpensive and more than <u>adequate</u>; in fact, with its large dining area, intimate fireplace, and big windows, the restaurant was in an ideal location. <u>Furthermore</u>, <u>revenue</u> did not appear to be a problem because Luigi's extended family operated many successful small businesses, and he knew that he could count on plenty of business from family connections. However, after a few months in operation, the restaurant failed. Unfortunately, Luigi had hired a cook who refused to do any <u>substitutions</u>. For instance, if a customer preferred pasta to rice, the cook got angry and yelled at the customer, telling him he had no appreciation of authentic Italian food. Since most people in the United States prefer to eat at restaurants that allow substitutions, Luigi's went out of business despite its marvelous location and a big potential source of revenue.

C. COMPREHENSION CHECK
Exercise 1

Refer to the previous reading and use the context to guess the meaning of the words below. Then match the words to their definitions. Do NOT use a dictionary.

___ 1. adequate	A.	connected to; affixed
___ 2. attached	B.	in addition; also
___ 3. revenue	C.	people or things that work or act in place of someone or something else
___ 4. substitution	D.	incoming money
___ 5. furthermore	E.	not bad, but not very good; enough

Exercise 2

True or False? Write T or F in the blanks provided.

___ 1. Soy can be used as a <u>substitute</u> for beef or pork.

___ 2. Agriculture is a major source of <u>revenue</u> for the U.S. economy.

___ 3. Your hands are <u>attached</u> to your legs.

___ 4. One hundred dollars a month is an <u>adequate</u> amount of money to live on in the USA.

___ 5. Speeding is against the law; <u>furthermore</u>, it is dangerous.

D. WORD STUDY
Exercise - Word Meanings

Most words have more than one meaning. Consider the meanings of the word **attach**.

1. attach (v) – to put something on, to affix
2. attach (v) – to affiliate with, associate with
3. attach (v) – to be in love with, emotionally dependent upon
4. attach (v) – to assign, attribute

Use either 1, 2, 3, or 4 to note which meaning is used in each sentence.

___ 1. I <u>attached</u> some digital photos to the electronic message I sent you.

___ 2. Lately, people have been <u>attaching</u> greater significance to minor problems.

___ 3. Sara cannot move away from San Francisco because she is too <u>attached</u> to the house she bought last year.

___ 4. The consular officer has been <u>attached</u> to the U.S. Embassy in Mexico for three years.

___ 5. Could you <u>attach</u> this worm to my hook?

___ 6. Little Johnny is <u>attached</u> to his old teddy bear.

E. USING WORDS IN COMMUNICATION

Exercise 1

Discuss these questions with a partner.

1. Are your living arrangements <u>adequate</u>?

2. Have you ever been emotionally <u>attached</u> to a physical object?

3. What is your primary source of <u>revenue</u>? Your parents? A job? Savings? A scholarship?

4. If you could <u>substitute</u> for a famous athlete, for whom would you like to play? Which sport would you play and why?

5. Tell your partner four reasons why you want to go to college. Use these connecting words:

   in addition   <u>furthermore</u>   moreover

Exercise 2

Cities and towns try to offer services to meet the needs of the people who live there (e.g., transportation, garbage collection). What services in your town (either your hometown or the town you live in now) are <u>adequate</u> and which services are <u>inadequate</u>? Make lists and then discuss them with a partner.

<u>Adequate Services</u>   <u>Inadequate Services</u>

REVIEW

Unscramble the sentences below.
The first sentence has been completed for you.

1. Service / the / Jack / by / Internal / audited / was / Revenue / .
   Jack was audited by the Internal Revenue Service.

2. ignored / model correctly / the / Because she / didn't build / Sara / the instructions, / the/ .
   _____

3. interesting / the economy / on / have an / Financial experts / perspective / .
   _____

4. needs dimensions / An architect / draft a blueprint / before she can / .
   _____

5. directions / adequate / were / weren't precise / His / but / , / they / .
   _____

6. the / We are / former welfare / monitoring / current status / of / recipients / .
   _____

7. is / beef / for / Fish / a / prime / poor substitute / .
   _____

8. I / I'm / you / you / divorcing / hate / ; / furthermore / .
   _____

9. consultation with the doctor / was / a / but / , / at full capacity / waiting room / the / I wanted / .
   _____

10. owning / Her mother's justification / for not buying the scooter / was that / one is / just a
    trend / .
    _____

11. are / photos / to / the / attached / e-mail / Digital / .
    _____

UNIT 7

WORDS

access	criteria	parallel	shift
accurate	discretion	principal	subsequent
concentration	implementation	promote	summary
consent	imposed	retain	undertake
coordination	marginal	scheme	volume

READINGS

Gymnastics
Minorities in Higher Education
Monitoring the Internet
The Xegan Appeal

STRATEGIES AND SKILLS

Word Forms
- Word family charts
- Word form selection

Comprehension Check
- Matching definitions
- Identifying synonyms
- Understanding and using words in context

Word Expansion
- Multiple meanings
- Collocations
- Grammar application

Interactive Speaking Practice
- Ranking skills
- Listing
- Associations
- Sentence completions
- Role play

ACADEMIC WORD POWER

LESSON 1

A. WORD FAMILIES
Study the five word families below. Then fill in the word form chart. The underlined word forms at the top of the list are the most commonly used forms in academic texts.

concentration	accurate	principal(2X)	undertake	coordination
/ˌkɑnsə'ntreɪʃən/	/'ækyərɪt/	/'prɪnsəpəl/	/ˌʌndər'teɪk/	/kouˌɔrdn'eɪʃən/
concentrate	accuracy	principally	undertaking	coordinate (2X)
	accurately			coordinator
	inaccuracy			
	inaccurate			
	inaccurately			

Exercise - Word Form Chart

NOUN	VERB	ADJECTIVE	ADVERB
1. concentration	1.		
1. 2.		1. accurate 2.	1. 2.
1.		1. principal	1.
1.	1. undertake		
1. coordination 2. 3.	1.		

B. READING

Gymnastics

The <u>principal</u> challenge for a gymnast is to hold her <u>concentration</u> while she attempts daring feats of physical skill. <u>Coordination</u> is also extremely important. A gymnast needs to be flexible, strong, graceful, and capable of remembering complicated movements. However, without concentration, she would fall from the balance beam or miss the vaulting horse. In order to achieve a high score from the judges, a gymnast must be <u>accurate</u> in her assessment of how fast and how far she needs to run in order to accomplish her somersaults or vaults. Finally, the gymnastics routines <u>undertaken</u> by the gymnast must be carefully executed with skill and precision so that she can perform them safely and possibly win a gold medal.

C. COMPREHENSION CHECK

Exercise 1

Refer to the previous reading and use the context to guess the meaning of the words below. Then match the words to their definitions. Do NOT use a dictionary.

___ 1. concentration   A. the ability to move the body well, basic athletic skill

___ 2. accurate   B. total attention to something

___ 3. coordination   C. tried, endeavored

___ 4. principal   D. main, most important

___ 5. undertaken   E. correct; able to hit a target

Exercise 2

True or False? Write T or F in the blanks provided.

___ 1. Professional basketball players don't have much <u>coordination</u>.

___ 2. The <u>principal</u> concern of a nation's president should be entertainment of the citizens.

___ 3. U.S. astronauts have <u>undertaken</u> many trips to the moon.

___ 4. In order to do good work, a great deal of <u>concentration</u> on a task is usually essential.

___ 5. Weathermen are always <u>accurate</u> in their predictions of weather patterns.

D. WORD STUDY

Exercise 1

Some words have more than one meaning. Consider the various meanings of the word **coordinate**.

1. coordinate (v) – to bring together various people and activities for a common purpose
2. coordinate (v) – to harmonize
3. coordinate (n) – a point of location on a map or graph

Use either 1, 2, or 3 to note which meaning is used in each sentence.

___ 1. The U.S. Air Force bombers accidentally hit the wrong target because they entered the wrong <u>coordinates</u> into their computers.

___ 2. A wedding planner <u>coordinates</u> all the various elements of a wedding.

___ 3. Academic administrators are responsible for <u>coordinating</u> their staff members so that each division's objectives can be met .

___ 4. Before their first child was born, they called in an expert designer who <u>coordinated</u> the decor of the baby's bedroom so that it would fit into the rest of the house.

Exercise 2
Choose the correct word form for each blank.

1. Most of the orange juice sold in grocery stores is made from water mixed with highly _____ orange juice.
   a. concentrate   b. concentration   c. concentrated

2. In order to be a good accountant, you need to perform mathematical calculations with a high level of _____.
   a. accurate   b. accuracy   c. accurately

3. The lead administrator of an American primary or secondary school is usually called the _____.
   a. principal   b. principally   c. principality

4. Designing a new shopping mall is a tremendous _____.
   a. undertaken   b. undertake   c. undertaking

5. A good _____ needs to be well-organized.
   a. coordination   b. coordinate   c. coordinator

E. USING WORDS IN COMMUNICATION
Exercise 1
Discuss the following.

1. Describe a major task that you have <u>undertaken</u> recently or will <u>undertake</u> in the future.
2. Are you <u>coordinated</u>? What sports do you play? Are you good at them? Is a great deal of <u>coordination</u> necessary for the sport that you like to play?
3. In your opinion, what is the <u>principal</u> reason that a person chooses a spouse?
4. Can you give an <u>accurate</u> assessment of the progress you have made in school? Do you think that your grades <u>accurately</u> reflect your ability?
5. Name at least three things that you do that require <u>concentration</u>.

Exercise 2
You and your partner are judges at an ice skating competition. You have to rank the skills necessary to win the competition. Put these skills in order, 1 being the principal consideration in judging and 4 being the least important.

_____ 1. difficulty of the routine <u>undertaken</u>
_____ 2. physical <u>coordination</u> of the athlete
_____ 3. amount of <u>concentration</u> evidenced in the routine
_____ 4. <u>accuracy</u> in the execution of the jumps and turns

LESSON 2

A. WORD FAMILIES

Study the five word families below. Then fill in the word form chart. The underlined word forms at the top of the list are the most commonly used forms in academic texts.

implementation	access (2X)	retain	volume	promote
/ˌɪmpləmənˈteɪʃən/	/ˈækˌsɛs/	/rəˈteɪn/	/ˈvɑlˌyum/	/prəˈmoʊt/
implement (2X)	accessible	retainer	voluminous	promoter
	accessibility	retention		promotion
	inaccessible	retentive		

Exercise - Word Form Chart

NOUN	VERB	ADJECTIVE	ADVERB
1. implementation 2.	1.		
1. access 2.	1.	1. 2.	
1. 2.	1. retain	1.	
1. volume		1.	
1. 2.	1. promote		

B. READING

Minorities in Higher Education

A primary means of increasing one's opportunities in the United States is by obtaining some form of higher education, that is, education beyond the secondary level, such as a university or college program. However, access to higher education is a controversial matter. Because of racial discrimination in the past, there had to be an <u>implementation</u> of special laws in order to ensure minorities a place in all institutions of higher education. Today, the high <u>volume</u> of minority students entering the university system is proof that <u>access</u> has increased. However, once those students are admitted, they must be <u>retained</u>. This is now the principal challenge for institutions of higher education. Once the minority students are attending school, how can they be kept at the institution? In addition, the students must not only be retained, they must also be <u>promoted</u> from year to year so that they graduate in a timely manner.

C. COMPREHENSION CHECK

Exercise 1

Refer to the previous reading and use the context to guess the meaning of the words below. Then match the words to their definitions. Do NOT use a dictionary.

___ 1. access
___ 2. implementation
___ 3. promoted
___ 4. volume
___ 5. retained

A. quantity, amount
B. advanced in rank
C. a way or means of reaching or entering a place
D. kept
E. the act of being put into action

Exercise 2

Which word does not belong?

1. access	admittance	right of entry	undertaking
2. implement	live	start	apply
3. promote	further	discourage	elevate
4. volume	amount	size	quality
5. retained	lost	held	owned

D. WORD STUDY

Exercise

Some words have more than one meaning. In some cases, the meanings are similar, but in some cases, they are not. Consider the definitions of the words below.

---
1. retain (v) - to keep or maintain possession of something

2. retain (v) - to pay a professional for services

---
3. volume (n) - a book or one of a series of books

4. volume (n) - intensity of sound

5. volume (n) - amount of activity

6. volume (n) - amount of space

Use either 1, 2, 3, 4, 5, or 6 to note which meaning is used in each sentence.

___ 1. Did you know that television stations always turn up the <u>volume</u> during commercials?
___ 2. Sam had to <u>retain</u> a lawyer when the police arrested him.
___ 3. The *Fellowship of the Ring* is the first <u>volume</u> in the *Lord of the Rings* trilogy by J.R.R. Tolkien.
___ 4. Many women <u>retain</u> water when they are pregnant.
___ 5. The <u>volume</u> of work for the post office goes way up in December.
___ 6. The dough for a loaf of bread should double in <u>volume</u> before you bake it.

E. USING WORDS IN COMMUNICATION
Exercise 1

1. List 3 <u>implements</u> that are used by painters.

2. List 3 products that are <u>promoted</u> on television.

3. List 3 appliances on which you can adjust the <u>volume</u>.

4. List 3 difficulties which might cause a student to be <u>retained</u> in a lower level class rather than <u>promoted</u> to the next higher level.

Exercise 2

To <u>implement</u> means to put into effect or to put into action. This word is frequently used when discussing rules and regulations. With a partner, think of some rules which should be <u>implemented</u> in your dormitory, apartment complex, or classroom. Discuss and then list them here.

LESSON 3

A. WORD FAMILIES

Study the five word families below. Then fill in the word form chart. The underlined word forms at the top of the list are the most commonly used forms in academic texts.

discretion	scheme (2X)	consent (2X)	subsequent	shift (2X)
/dɪˈskrɛʃən/	/skim/	/kənˈsɛnt/	/ˈsʌbsəkwənt/	/ʃɪft/
discreet	schematic (2X)	consenting	subsequently	
discreetly	schematically	consensus		
discretionary				
indiscreet				
indiscretion				

Exercise - Word Form Chart

NOUN	VERB	ADJECTIVE	ADVERB
1. discretion 2.		1. 2. 3.	1.
1. scheme 2.	1.	1.	1.
1. 2.	1. consent	1.	
		1. subsequent	1.
1. shift	1.		

B. READING

Monitoring the Internet

Although the Internet has revolutionized our lives, making information much more easily accessible to everyone with a computer, it has also resulted in easy access to pornography. This creates a big problem for the parents of children and teenagers with computers. Parents think that what their children look at should be subject to parental <u>discretion</u>, and the Internet makes it difficult for parents to monitor the images that their children watch. Most parents will not <u>consent</u> to having their children look at images of naked men and women, but there are <u>schemes</u> on the Internet which not only expose the children to porn but, in some cases, recruit children for the porn industry. When the Internet first became popular, there was widespread opposition to governmental monitoring of the Internet. However, there was a <u>subsequent</u> <u>shift</u> in public opinion after several pornography rings were exposed.

C. COMPREHENSION CHECK
Exercise 1
Refer to the previous reading and use the context to guess the meaning of the words below. Then match the words to their definitions. Do NOT use a dictionary.

___ 1. scheme	A. secret or dishonest plans; a plots
___ 2. discretion	B. a change in position
___ 3. consent	C. good judgment; caution
___ 4. shift	D. happening later
___ 5. subsequent	E. to agree to something

Exercise 2
Fill in the blank using the appropriate vocabulary word

1. Earthquakes occur whenever there is a _____ in the tectonic plates.

2. Driving manuals urge drivers to use their _____ when passing other cars on a busy highway.

3. Sondra was relieved when her child was finally born. However, she was surprised at the _____ birth of her second child, an unexpected twin!

4. The old woman was dismayed to learn that there had been a _____ invented to make her buy an expensive product that she really did not need.

5. Soldiers must obtain written _____ from their commanding officers if they wish to take a leave of absence from their duties.

D. WORD STUDY
Exercise

These are some common collocations for words in this unit.

parental discretion	consenting adults	classification scheme
subsequent generations	discretionary spending	

Circle the letter of the correct answers for these collocations.

1. Which of the following activities need not be subject to <u>parental discretion</u>?

   a. children watching television

   b. children playing computer games

   c. children painting pictures in their pre-school classrooms

2. What activities should only take place between <u>consenting adults</u>?

   a. sexual acts

   b. playing football and basketball

   c. credit card transactions

3. Which of the following have **not** been placed in a <u>classification scheme</u>?

   a. plants

   b. tissue papers

   c. animals

4. What kind of institution is created with the interests of <u>subsequent generations</u> in mind?

   a. schools

   b. nightclubs

   c. restaurants

5. Lawmakers are allowed to use <u>discretionary spending</u> for what purpose?

   a. redecorating their homes in Washington, D.C.

   b. paying down interest on the national debt

   c. purchasing new yachts for their weekend excursions

E. USING WORDS IN COMMUNICATION

Exercise 1

In the chart below, write one word you associate with each of the words from this lesson. Then go around the classroom and see if anyone has one or more of the same words associated with the vocabulary words. If you find someone who does, sit with that classmate and discuss your associations. If you do not find a student with any of the same associations, choose a partner with whom to discuss your associations.

discretion	
scheme	
consent	
subsequent	
shift	

Exercise 2

Repeat and complete the following sentences:

1. I try to be <u>discreet</u> about ...

2. I learned about this <u>scheme</u> on the news. It involved...

3. If someone needed my <u>consent</u> to execute a prisoner, I would say...

4. <u>Subsequent</u> to getting engaged, most people...

5. I may <u>shift</u> my position on the following issue...

LESSON 4

A. WORD FAMILIES

Study the five word families below. Then fill in the word form chart. The underlined word forms at the top of the list are the most commonly used forms in academic texts.

impose	criteria	marginal	parallel (3X)	summary
/ɪmˈpoʊz/	/kraɪˈtiriə/	/ˈmɑrdʒənəl/	/ˈpærəˌlɛl/	/ˈsʌməri/
imposing	criterion	margin	paralleled	summarize
imposition		marginally	unparalleled	summarization

Exercise - Word Form Chart

NOUN	VERB	ADJECTIVE	ADVERB
1.	1. impose	1.	
1. criteria 2.			
1.		1. marginal	1.
1.	1.	1. parallel 2. 3.	
1. summary 2.	1.		

B. READING

The Xegan Appeal

When Steve Johnson wrote a science fiction short story about life in a parallel universe, critics showed only marginal interest in the story. However, after it was published in several science fiction fan magazines, the story grew in popularity. This is a summary of the story. An alien race colonized the planet XegXeg and imposed slavery upon the human-like creatures, the Xegans, who lived there. The Xegans were unhappy, to say the least. They argued with the colonists, saying that the criteria by which the Xegans were judged by the aliens were unfair. How could a so-called more-advanced civilization justify enslaving a race of peaceful creatures such as the Xegans? Through their skillful negotiations with the aliens, the Xegans were ultimately freed from their oppressors after continuous nonviolent protest. Today, Johnson's story is in competition for one of the top ten science fiction short stories of the year.

C. COMPREHENSION CHECK
Exercise 1
Refer to the reading above and use the context to guess the meaning of the words below. Then match the words to their definitions. Do NOT use a dictionary.

___ 1. imposed	A.	rules used to judge something, standard of measurement
___ 2. criteria	B.	a brief statement of the most important features of an event or work
___ 3. marginal	C.	of little importance or worth
___ 4. parallel	D.	placed upon, forced upon
___ 5. summary	E.	similar, bearing a likeness to

Exercise 2
Is the vocabulary word used correctly in the following sentences? Write Yes if the word is used correctly or No if the word is used incorrectly.

___ 1. The press considered the birth of the new princess of <u>marginal</u> interest to the readers, so they published the story on the last page.

___ 2. Organic chemistry is <u>parallel</u> to art history.

___ 3. The monarch <u>imposed</u> a new tax on the citizens of his land.

___ 4. Lions use several <u>criteria</u> to eat their prey.

___ 5. The newspaper article included a <u>summary</u> of the events leading up to the explosion.

D. WORD STUDY
Exercise 1
Find and correct the errors in the following sentences.

1. Meredith saw her in-laws' month-long visit as an impose.

   (1 mistake)

2. Teachers use many criterion to evaluate there students' performance.

   (2 mistakes)

3. English instructors are always write in the marginal of their students' papers.

   (2 mistakes)

4. The magnitude of the attack was unparallelling in the history of the country.

   (1 mistake)

5. Graduate students must be able to summary their dissertation research in less than thirty pages.

   (1 mistake)

Exercise 2
Most words have more than one meaning. Consider the various meanings of the word **parallel**.

---

1. parallel (v) - to be similar or to occur at the same time

2. parallel (n) - a likeness or connection between two or more events

3. parallel (adj) - running side by side at an equal distance apart

---

Use either 1, 2, or 3 to note which meaning is used in each sentence.

___ 1. Lines which are truly <u>parallel</u> never meet.

___ 2. His accident <u>paralleled</u> that of his sister, who lived on the opposite coast.

___ 3. Detectives could see a distinct <u>parallel</u> between the two murders.

___ 4. Gymnasts perform on <u>parallel</u> wooden bars.

E. USING WORDS IN COMMUNICATION
Exercise 1
Role Play - You and your partner are English teachers. You are discussing your students' writing. Write a dialog using all five vocabulary words (i.e., **imposed, criteria, marginal, parallel, summary**). Be prepared to perform your dialog for the class.

Exercise 2

1. List 3 <u>parallels</u> between your family and your partner's family.

2. List 3 <u>criteria</u> you use to judge a potential boyfriend or girlfriend, or spouse.

3. List 3 <u>marginally</u> famous people.

4. List 3 ways in which a culture has <u>imposed</u> itself upon another.
   (For example, the British imposed their system of government on many conquered nations.)

5. List 3 movies which tell stories you could <u>summarize</u> in less than 60 seconds.

REVIEW

The crossword puzzle on the following page contains all 20 words from Unit 7. Solve the puzzle by filling in the blanks to complete the sentences.

The crossword puzzle contains all 20 words from Unit 7.
Solve the puzzle by filling in the blanks to complete the sentences.

ACROSS

6. The panel of judges must agree on the _____ they will use to judge the competition

7. We could not hear the program, so we asked the attendant to turn up the _____ .

9. My little brother had to be _____ in the second grade because he had not yet learned to read.

11. The attorney lost his first major case, but _____ victories ensured his professional success.

14. Her boss would like to _____ her, but she seems to lack the ambition necessary for top management.

15. A communist government was _____ upon the Czechoslovakians after World War II.

16. Several laws were passed but there was never any _____ of the resulting regulations.

19. Children in many cultures cannot marry without their parents' _____ .

DOWN

1. The lawyer did not have time to read the entire document, so she asked her assistant to write a _____ of the paper.

2. Chess is a game that requires a high level of _____ . You must think long and hard before you move.

3. In order to understand certain geometry equations, you must remember that _____ lines are lines that never touch each other.

4. I did not have _____ to the high security section of the chemistry lab.

5. Since winter set in, there has been a noticeable _____ in the weather patterns.

6. Few people have the _____ of Michael Jordan. As a result, most people are much less graceful and athletic than the superstar.

8. Many great projects have been _____ over the years.

10. Many television networks advise viewer _____ when the content of a program is violent or sexual in content.

12. In 1999, they launched the _____ that would make them rich beyond their wildest dreams, but by 2001, the police had busted them.

13. Their _____ concern was saving as many people from the rubble as quickly as they could find them. Nothing was more important to the rescuers.

17. James made only _____ improvement in his French class this semester because he didn't study very much and rarely spoke French outside of class.

18. We need an _____ count of how many employees will attend the company party. Without one, we cannot know how much food to buy.

APPENDICES

A. ACADEMIC WORD LIST INDEX
B. ROOTS, PREFIXES, SUFFIXES

APPENDIX A
WORD LIST INDEX

Academic Word List Index

The 140 target words studied in this book come from the Academic Word List (see Introduction, page ix for a description of the AWL). The four volumes of Academic Word Power cover 560 of the 570 words on the AWL. Below is a complete, alphabetical list of the AWL. The numbers indicate the volume, unit and page number where the word is introduced.

Word	v.u.pg	Word	v.u.pg	Word	v.u.pg
abandon	3.7.90	aspect	1.5.65	coincide	4.4.51
abstract	3.3.40	assemble	4.2.18	collapse	4.6.78
academy	2.2.18	assess	1.6.85	colleague	4.1.2
access	2.7.92	assign	3.7.101	commence	4.5.64
accommodate	4.5.70	assist	1.1.8	comment	3.7.96
accompany	3.7.101	assume	3.1.5	commission	1.6.76
accumulate	4.1.8	assure	4.6.78	commitment	2.5.75
accurate	2.7.94	attach	2.6.89	commodity	4.6.81
achieve	1.2.18	attain	4.2.24	communicate	
acknowledge	3.4.46	attitude	2.2.21	community	1.1.2
acquire	1.7.100	attribute	3.1.5	compatible	4.5.60
adapt	3.6.84	author	2.5.75	compensate	2.2.24
adequate	2.6.89	authority	1.4.46	compile	4.5.64
adjacent	4.4.46	automate	3.3.32	complement	4.7.96
adjust	2.5.66	available	1.1.8	complex	1.4.53
administrate	1.4.46	aware	2.4.56	component	4.1.11
adult	3.2.24	behalf	4.5.70	compound	4.3.35
advocate	3.4.46	benefit	1.1.8	comprehensive	3.4.49
affect	1.2.18	bias	3.3.34	comprise	3.5.66
aggregate	3.5.60	bond	4.1.2	compute	1.4.56
aid	3.2.24	brief	2.5.69	conceive	4.7.90
albeit	4.7.99	bulk	4.3.32	concentrate	2.7.94
allocate	3.6.81	capable	3.2.18	concept	1.3.41
alter	2.1.8	capacity	2.6.86	conclude	1.1.11
alternative	2.3.37	category	1.5.71	concurrent	4.7.90
ambiguous	3.4.52	cease	4.4.46	conduct	1.7.90
amend	3.1.8	challenge	2.1.5	confer	4.1.11
analogy	4.4.48	channel	4.1.8	confine	4.6.76
analyze	1.5.68	chapter	1.2.18	confirm	3.3.32
annual	2.1.11	chart	4.3.40	conflict	3.1.2
anticipate	4.1.11	chemical	4.2.18	conform	3.4.52
apparent	2.4.60	circumstance	2.2.21	consent	2.7.100
append	4.3.32	cite	3.4.46	consequent	1.7.93
appreciate	3.2.24	civil	2.5.69	considerable	2.4.50
approach	1.2.18	clarify	3.6.81	consist	1.4.46
appropriate	1.3.32	classic	4.3.32	constitute	
approximate	2.2.28	clause	2.4.60	constant	2.3.43
arbitrary	4.3.38	code	4.2.21	contract	1.5.71
area	1.1.11	coherent	4.6.76	constrain	3.1.8

Word	v.u.pg	Word	v.u.pg	Word	v.u.pg
constrain	1.6	differentiate	3.6.74	evaluate	1.2.21
consult	2.6.86	dimension	2.6.86	eventual	3.4.52
consume	1.3.32	diminish	4.3.35	evident	1.3.38
contact	4.3.32	discrete	2.7.100	evolve	2.4.57
contemporary	3.3.34	discriminate	3.4.52	exceed	3.3.32
context	1.218	displace	4.5.70	exclude	1.7.90
contradict	3.5.66	display	2.5.75	exhibit	3.7.97
contrary	4.2.21	dispose	3.6.77	expand	4.3.40
contrast	2.2.24	distinct	1.4.50	expert	2.6.83
contribute	2.3.40	distort	4.7.93	explicit	3.5.63
controversy	4.7.93	distribute	1.5.68	exploit	4.6.76
convene	2.5.75	diverse	3.3.34	export	1.5.71
converse	4.1.2	document	1.7.93	external	2.3.46
convert	3.6.84	domain	3.5.60	extract	3.6.77
convince	4.4.46	domestic	2.4.53	facilitate	4.3.32
cooperate	3.2.27	dominate	2.3.37	factor	1.1.2
coordinate	2.2.94	draft	2.6.86	feature	1.4.50
core	1.7.100	drama	3.7.90	federal	4.2.27
corporate	4.2.24	duration	4.2.27	fee	2.5.66
correspond	2.3.43	dynamic	3.4.55	file	4.1.5
couple		economy	1.4.50	final	1.1.14
create	1.2.21	edit	3.5.69	finance	1.5.62
credit	1.3.32	element	1.3.41	finite	3.6.77
criteria	2.7.104	eliminate	3.2.21	flexible	2.5.75
crucial	3.4.49	emerge	2.3.34	fluctuate	3.7.97
culture	1.1.2	emphasis	1.2.21	focus	1.3.32
currency	4.4.54	empirical	3.6.74	format	4.4.51
cycle	2.2.21	enable	4.1.5	formula	1.7.100
data	1.3.35	encounter	4.3.40	forthcoming	4.5.84
debate	2.2.18	energy	2.1.2	foundation	3.3.37
decade	3.2.21	enforce	3.1.2	found	4.3.40
decline	2.4.50	enhance	3.3.34	framework	2.2.28
deduce	2.2.28	enormous	4.4.54	function	1.5.68
define	1.1.11	ensure	2.1.5	fund	1.7.93
definite	3.6.77	entity	4.2.18	fundamental	2.3.37
demonstrate	2.1.5	environment	1.1.5	furthermore	2.6.89
denote	4.2.27	equate	1.6.82	gender	3.2.18
deny	3.2.18	equip	3.2.21	generate	3.1.11
depress	4.6.76	equivalent	2.5.72	generation	2.2.28
derived	3.1.5	erode	4.4.46	globe	3.3.34
design	1.3.35	error	2.2.24	goal	2.1.8
despite	2.1.8	establish	1.6.79	grade	4.2.21
detect	3.7.94	estate		grant	2.4.57
deviate	4.4.51	estimate	1.5.62	guarantee	3.2.18
device	4.5.64	ethic	4.3.40	guideline	3.3.32
devoted	4.6.78	ethnic	2.4.53	hence	4.1.8

Word	v.u.pg	Word	v.u.pg	Word	v.u.pg
hierarchy	3.6.74	internal	2.2.24	minimum	2.5.69
highlight	3.2.27	interpret	1.4.56	ministry	4.1.2
hypothesis	2.5.72	interval	3.5.66	minor	1.1.5
identical	3.2.24	intervene	3.4.46	mode	3.4.55
ideology	3.7.90	intrinsic	4.6.81	modify	2.3.43
ignorance	2.6.83	invest	1.7.93	monitor	2.6.80
illustrate	2.1.11	investigate	2.3.43	motive	3.1.2
image	2.3.37	invoke	4.6.81	mutual	4.7.90
immigrate	2.2.21	involve	1.2.24	negate	1.6.79
impact	1.5.62	isolate	3.1.8	network	2.4.53
implement	2.7.97	issue	1.7.100	neutral	3.3.40
implicate	4.2.27	item	1.4.50	nevertheless	3.1.5
implicit	4.7.90	job	2.1.8	nonetheless	4.4.54
imply	2.1.11	journal	1.6.79	norm	4.4.51
impose	2.7.104	justify	2.6.83	normal	1.1.5
incentives	3.5.60	label	2.1.2	notion	2.5.72
incidence	3.6.74	labor	1.6.85	notwithstanding	4.7.90
incline	4.7.99	layer	1.7.96	nuclear	4.6.78
income	1.6.76	lecture	2.5.72	objective	2.4.60
incorporate	3.6.74	legal	1.453	obtain	1.5.68
index	4.1.5	legislate	1.5.65	obvious	2.2.24
indicate	1.4.46	levy	4.5.64	occupy	2.2.18
individual	1.2.21	liberal	2.5.66	occur	1.1.5
induce	4.5.60	license	2.3.40	odd	4.5.60
inevitable	4.5.70	likewise	4.2.18	offset	4.7.96
infer	3.2.24	link	1.7.96	ongoing	4.3.38
infrastructure	4.6.78	locate	1.6.82	option	2.3.46
inherent	4.4.48	logic	2.4.57	orient	2.5.66
inhibit	3.6.84	maintain	1.3.38	outcome	2.1.5
initial	1.7.90	major	1.2.24	output	
initiate	3.5.69	manipulate	3.7.94	overall	2.4.57
innovate	3.3.37	manual	4.4.46	overlap	4.4.54
input		margin	2.7.104	overseas	4.1.2
insert	3.7.101	mature	4.3.35	panel	4.2.21
insight	4.3.38	maximize	1.6.82	paradigm	4.1.11
inspect	3.3.32	mechanism	4.2.18	paragraph	
instance	2.4.60	media	3.2.21	parallel	2.7.104
institute	1.5.65	mediate	4.7.93	parameter	3.1.8
instruct	2.6.86	medical	2.3.34	participate	1.1.2
integral	4.7.96	medium	4.3.35	partner	1.2.24
integrate	2.4.50	mental	2.1.11	passive	4.5.70
integrity	4.2.21	method	1.1.8	perceive	1.6.76
intelligence	2.5.69	migrate	3.1.11	percent	1.2.24
intense	3.7.97	military	4.5.60	period	1.5.71
interact	1.3.38	minimal	4.6.81	persist	4.6.76
intermediate		minimize	3.2.21	perspective	2.6.86

Word	v.u.pg	Word	v.u.pg	Word	v.u.pg
phase	2.2.28	recover	3.1.10	simulate	3.4.55
phenomenon	3.4.55	refine	4.5.67	site	1.7.90
philosophy	1.7.96	regime	4.2.27	so-called	4.5.67
physical	1.1.5	region	1.3.41	sole	3.2.18
plus	4.2.24	register	1.7.96	somewhat	3.4.52
policy	1.3.41	regulate	1.5.65	source	2.1.2
portion	4.3.35	reinforce	3.7.101	specific	1.4.53
pose	4.5.67	reject	2.3.34	specify	4.6.84
positive	1.3.32	relax	4.1.5	sphere	4.2.24
potential	1.6.76	release	3.5.60	stable	2.5.66
practitioner	4.7.99	relevant	1.6.82	statistic	2.5.72
precede	3.3.40	reluctance	4.3.38	status	2.6.80
precise	2.6.80	rely	1.4.50	straightforward	4.6.84
predict	2.1.5	remove	1.4.56	strategy	1.5.62
predominant	3.7.90	require	1.2.27	stress	2.1.2
preliminary	4.4.51	research	1.4.53	structure	1.4.56
presume	3.4.49	reside	1.5.65	style	2.3.37
previous	1.4.46	resolve	2.4.50	submit	3.6.81
primary	1.5.71	resource	1.4.53	subordinate	4.5.60
prime	2.6.80	restrain	4.6.84	subsequent	2.7.100
principal	2.7.94	restrict	1.7.93	subsidy	3.5.66
principle	1.4.56	retain	2.7.97	substitute	2.6.89
prior	3.3.37	reveal	3.1.5	successor	3.3.40
proceed	4.6.84	revenue	2.6.89	sufficient	2.4.57
process	1.2.24	reverse	3.5.63	sum	2.3.40
professional	2.1.2	revise	3.6.81	summary	2.7.104
prohibit	3.5.63	revolution	4.4.48	supplement	4.4.54
project	2.3.34	revise	3.6.81	survey	1.3.35
promote	2.7.97	role	1.6.76	survive	3.5.69
proportion	2.4.53	route	4.7.99	suspend	4.7.93
prospect	3.6.84	scenario	4.7.96	sustain	2.3.34
protocol	4.7.99	schedule	3.2.27	symbol	2.4.60
psychology		scheme	2.7.100	tape	4.1.5
publication	3.5.66	scope	3.6.81	target	2.1.11
publish	2.2.18	section	1.2.27	task	1.2.27
purchase	1.5.62	sector	1.6.85	team	4.2.24
pursue	2.5.69	secure	1.3.38	technical	4.1.8
qualitative	4.6.81	seek	1.6.82	technique	1.7.90
quote	3.3.37	select	1.3.35	technology	1.3.38
radical	3.7.90	sequence	1.7.100	temporary	4.3.38
random	3.2.27	sex		tense	3.4.46
range	1.6.79	series	2.1.8	terminate	3.6.84
ratio	3.1.8	shift	2.7.100	text	1.3.35
rational	3.4.49	significance	1.3.41	theme	3.7.94
react	1.6.85	similar	1.1.11	theory	1.6.79

Word	v.u.pg
thereby	3.7.101
thesis	3.2.27
topic	3.5.69
trace	3.6.77
tradition	1.2.27
transfer	1.5.68
transform	3.4.55
transit	2.3.43
transmit	3.5.63
transport	3.1.11
trend	2.6.83
trigger	4.7.93
ultimate	3.5.63
undergo	4.4.48
underlie	3.1.2
undertake	2.7.94
uniform	3.7.97
unify	4.5.67
unique	3.3.40
utilize	3.1.11
valid	2.2.18
vary	1.2.27
vehicle	3.7.94
version	2.4.53
via	3.7.94
violate	4.6.84
virtual	3.7.97
visible	3.5.80
vision	4.5.67
visual	4.1.8
volume	2.7.97
voluntary	3.5.69
welfare	2.6.83
whereas	4.1.11
whereby	4.7.96
widespread	3.4.49

APPENDIX B
Roots, Prefixes, Suffixes

COMMON ROOTS, PREFIXES AND SUFFIXES IN ACADEMIC VOCABULARY

Academic vocabulary is mainly of Latin or Greek origin, so knowing common Greek and Latin roots, prefixes, and suffixes can be very helpful in learning and remembering academic vocabulary. The following tables list some common roots and affixes along with their meanings and examples. The examples in bold are words from the Academic Word List.

LATIN ROOTS

Roots	Meaning	Examples
act	to do, drive	**interact, compact, extract**
ann, enn	year	**annual,** bicentennial
aqu	water	aquarium, aqueduct
aud	to hear	auditorium, auditor
bell	war	belligerent, bellicose
cede	to go, to yield	**precede,** concede
cent	one hundred	**percent,** centennial
cept, capt, cip, cap, ceive, ceipt	to take hold, grasp	**conceive,** receive, capture
cert	to be sure, to trust	certain, certify
cess, ced	to go, to yield	**process, successor,** cessation
cid, cis	to cut off, be brief, to kill	concise, homicide
circ, circum	around	**circumstance,** circumference
clin	to lean, lie, bend	**decline, incline**
cog	to think, consider	recognize, cognitive
cor, cord, card	heart	coronary, cardiology
corp	body	**corporate,** corpse
cred	to believe, to trust	**credit,** credible
crit, cris	to separate, judge	**criteria ,** criticism
culp	fault, blame	culprit, culpable
dic, dict	to say, to speak, to assert	**contradict, predict**
duct, duc	to lead, to draw	**conduct, deduce**
dur	hard, lasting	**duration,** durable
ego	I	egotistical, egocentric
equ	equal, fair	**equation,** equator
fac, fic, fect, fact	to make, do	**facilitate, affect**
fer	to carry, bear, bring	**transfer, infer, confer**
fin	end, limit	**definite, finite, confine**
flu	to flow	**fluctuations,** fluid
form	shape	**uniform , formula, transform**
fort	strong	fortify, fortress
fum	smoke, scent	perfume, fumigate
gen	race, family, kind	**generation, gender**
grad, gress	step, degree, rank	**grade,** gradual
grat	pleasing, thankful	grateful, congratulate
grav, griev	heavy	gravity, grieve, grave
hab	to have, hold, to dwell	habitat, habit
hom	man, human	homicide, homage
init	to begin, enter upon	**initial, initiate**
jur, jus, judic	law, right, judgment	**justify, adjust,** judicial
juven	young	juvenile, rejuvenate
laud	praise	laud, laudable
leg	law	**legal, legislate**
liber	free	**liberal, liberate**

Roots	Meaning	Examples
loc	place	**location, allocate,** local
manu	hand	**manual,** manuscript
med, medi	middle	**medium, mediate,** mediocre
medic	physician, to heal	**medical,** medicine
memor	mindful	memorial, memorable
mon	to remind, advise, warn	**monitor, demonstrate**
ment	mind	**mental,** mentality
migr	to move, travel	**immigration, migration**
mit, mis	to send	**transmit,** submit
mort	death	mortal, mortality
mov, mob, mot	to move	**remove,** mobile, motion
mut	change, exchange	mutate, mutant
nomen, nomin	name, meaning	nominate, synonym
null, nihil, nil	nothing, void	nihilism, nullify
ped	foot	pedestrian, pedestal
pend, pond, pens	to weigh, pay, to consider	**compensate,** pension, pensive
plur, plus	more	**plus,** surplus
port	to carry	**export, transport**
pos	to place, put	**dispose, impose, expose**
pot	powerful	**potential,** potent
prim, prin	first	**primary, prime**
reg, rig, rect	to rule, right, straight	**regulation,** rigid
rupt	to break, burst	disrupt, interrupt, rupture
sacr, secr, sanct	sacred	sacrifice, sanctify
sat, satis	enough	satisfy, satiate
scrib, script	to write	inscribe, subscription
sed, sid, sess	to sit, to settle	sedate, sediment, subside
sent, sens	to feel	sentimental, sense
sequ, secut	to follow, sequence	**consequence, sequence, subsequent**
sumil, simul, sembl	like,	**similar, simulation**
sol, soli	alone, lonely	**solely, isolate**
spec, spect, spic	to see, look at, behold	**perspective, inspect**
spond, spons	to pledge, promise	**respond, correspond**
tac, tic	silent	tacit, taciturn
ten, tain, tent	to hold	**obtain, retain, attain**
tend, tens	to stretch, strive	**tension,** tendon
termin	boundary, limit	**terminate, terminal**
test	to witness, affirm	attest, testify
tract	to pull, draw	**contract, extract**
trib	to allot, give	**distribute, contribute**
vac	empty	evacuate, vacuous
ven, vent	to come	**convention, intervene**
ver	truth	verify, veracity
vers, vert	to turn	**convert, reverse, controversy**
via	way, road	**via,** viaduct
vir	manliness, worth	virile, virtue
vis, vid	to see, look	**visible, revision, visual**
viv, vit	life	vital, vivacious
voc, vok	voice, call	**invoke, vocal, revoke**

Roots	Meaning	Examples
GREEK ROOTS		
anthropo	human being	anthropology, philanthropic
aster, astro	star	asteroid, astronomy
bio	life	biography, biology
chrom	color	chromatic, chromosome
chrono	time	chronology, chronometer
cosmo	world, order, universe	cosmos, cosmopolitan
crac, crat	rule, govern	aristocrat, democracy
dem	people	**demonstrate,** epidemic
derm	skin	dermatology, hypodermic
ethno	nation	ethnic, ethnocentric
eu	good, well	euphoric, euphemism
gam	marriage	monogamy, polygamy
geo	earth	geology, geodynamics
gno, kno	to know	knowledge, diagnostic
graph gram	to write, draw, record	telegraph, telegram
gymno, gymn	athletic	gymnasium, gymnastics
hydro	water	hydrogen, hydroplane
hypno	sleep	hypnosis, hypnotize
hypo	under, below	**hypothesis,** hypodermic
logue, logo	idea, word, speech, reason	**logic, ideological**
meter, metr	measure	**parameters,** metric
micro	small	microscope, microorganism
mim	copy	mimic, mime
mono	one	monogram, monogamy
mor	fool	moron, moronic
morph	form, structure, shape	morphology, metamorphosis
neur, nero	nerve	neural, neurotic
opt	eye	optic, optician
ortho	straight	orthodontist, orthopedics
pan	all	**expansion,** pantheism
path	feeling, disease	sympathy, pathologist
phe	speak, spoken about	prophet, euphemistic
phil, philo	love	**philosophy,** philanthropist
phob	fear	phobia, claustrophobia
phon	sound, voice	telephone, phonograph
photo	light	photosynthesis, photography
pneu	breath	pneumonia, pneumatic
polis, polit	citizen, city, state	political, metropolitan
poly	many	polygamy, polytechnic
pseudo	false	pseudo, pseudonym
psych	mind, soul, spirit	psychic, psychology
pyr	fire	pyromania, pyrotechnic
scope	to see	**scope,** telescope
soph	wise	**philosophy,** sophisticated
sym, syn	together	**symbolic,** synthesize
techn	art, skill	**technical, technology**
tele	at a distance	telescope, telephone
the, them, thet	to place, put	**hypothesis,** epithet
thea, theatr	to see, view	theatre, theatrical
theo	God	**theory,** theology
therm	heat	thermometer, thermal

PREFIXES

Prefix	Meaning	Examples
ab-	from, away from	absent, **abnormal**
ad-	to, motion toward, addition to	**advocate, administrate, adapt**
aero-	air	aerobic, aerospace
a-, an-	without	atonal, anarchy
ante-	before	antecedent, anteroom
anti-	against, opposite, reverse	anti-aircraft, antibiotics
ap-	to, nearness to	**approximate**, appoint
auto-	self	**automatic**, autograph
bene-	good	**benefit**, benefactor
bi-	two	**biannual**, bifocal
co-, con-	together	**community, cooperative, coordination , context**
contra-	against	**contrast, controversy, contradiction**
de-	opposite of, away from, undo	**deduction, decline**
dis-	opposite	**displace, disproportion**
ex-	out, beyond, away from, former	**exclude, export, external**
extra-	outside, beyond, besides	extraordinary, extracurricular
fore-	before	foreword, forecast
hyper-	more than normal, too much	hyperactive, hypersensitive
il-	not	**illegal, illogical**
im-	into	**impact, imply, immigrate**
im-	not	**immature**, imbalance
in-	not	**incapable, indiscreet, inaccurate**
inter-	among, between	**interaction, intervention, interval**
intra-	within	intramural, intrastate
ir-	not	**irrelevant, irrational**
mal-	wrong, bad	malfunction, malpractice
mis-	wrong, bad, no, not	misinterpret, misbehave
non-	not, opposite of	nontraditional, nonconformist
per-	through	**perceive, perspective**
post-	after	postgraduate, postglacial
pre-	before	**precede, previous, preliminary**
pro-	before, for, in support of	**promote**, prologue
pro-	forward	**project, proceed**
re-	back, again	**reassess, recreate, redefine**
retro-	backward	retroactive, retrospect
self-	of the self	self-respect, self-taught
semi-	half, partly	semiformal, semi-circle
sub-	under, beneath	**subordinate**, submarine
sur-	over, above	surcharge, surpass, **survey**
trans-	across, over	**transition, transport**
ultra-	extremely	ultramodern, ultrasonic
un-	not, lack of, opposite	**uninvolved, unreliable, unaware**

SUFFIXES

Suffix	Meaning	Examples
-able, -ible	can, able to	detectable, accessible, flexible
-age	action or process	percentage, linkage, voyage
-al, -ial	of, like, relating to, suitable for	cultural, traditional, potential
-ance	act, process, quality, state of being	maintenance, reliance, assurance
-ant	one who	assistant, participant
-ary	of, like, relating to	temporary, primary, voluntary
-ate	characteristic of, to become	alternate, demonstrate, eliminate
-cle, -icle	small	particle, cubicle
-cy	fact, or state of being	policy, residency
-dom	state or quality of	random, boredom
-ence	act or state of being	evidence, sequence, intelligence
-ent	doing, having, showing	consistent, sufficient, inherent
-er	one who, that which	consumer, achiever
-ery	place for, act, practice of	recovery, robbery
-ess	female	princess, goddess
-ful	full of	stressful, insightful
-ic	relating to, characteristic of	economic, specific, academic
-ify	to make, to cause to be	identify, unify
-ion	act, condition, result of,	conclusion, evaluation
-ish	of or belonging to, characterized by	stylish, selfish
-ism	act, practice, or result of, example	individualism, professionalism
-ity	condition, state of being	security, maturity, stability
-ive	of, relating to, belonging to	negative, alternative, legislative
-ize	make, cause to be, subject to	civilize, energize, finalize
-less	without	ceaseless, jobless
-logue	speech	dialogue, monologue
-logy	study or theory of	psychology, ideology
-ly	every	annually, daily
-ly	in (a specified manner, to a specified extent)	normally, automatically
-ment	action or process	commitment, assessment, adjustment
-ment	state or quality of	refinement, amusement
-ment	product or thing	environment, document
-ness	state or quality of being	awareness, uniqueness, intenseness
-or	one who	minor, actor
-ous	having, full of, characterized by	ambiguous, enormous, erroneous
-ship	state or quality of being	partnership, authorship
-some	like, tending to be	bothersome, noisome
-tude	state of quality of being	attitude, solitude
-y	characterized by	contemporary, voluntary, contrary

Reference:
Elliot, Norbert. Vocabulary Workshop. Austin, Texas: Holt, Rinehart and Winston, 2001.

CPSIA information can be obtained
at www.ICGtesting.com
Printed in the USA
FFOW04n0941181117
43574419-42352FF